THREE TIMES *the* LOVE

AVERY

a member of Penguin Group (USA) Inc.

New York

THREE
TIMES
the
LOVE

• • •

Finding Answers and Hope
for Our Triplets with Autism

LYNN AND RANDY GASTON

Published by the Penguin Group
Penguin Group (USA) Inc., 375 Hudson Street, New York, New York 10014, USA • Penguin Group (Canada),
90 Eglinton Avenue East, Suite 700, Toronto, Ontario M4P 2Y3, Canada (a division of Pearson Penguin
Canada Inc.) • Penguin Books Ltd, 80 Strand, London WC2R 0RL, England • Penguin Ireland,
25 St Stephen's Green, Dublin 2, Ireland (a division of Penguin Books Ltd) • Penguin Group (Australia),
250 Camberwell Road, Camberwell, Victoria 3124, Australia (a division of Pearson Australia Group Pty Ltd) •
Penguin Books India Pvt Ltd, 11 Community Centre, Panchsheel Park, New Delhi–110 017,
India • Penguin Group (NZ), 67 Apollo Drive, Rosedale, North Shore 0632, New Zealand (a division
of Pearson New Zealand Ltd) • Penguin Books (South Africa) (Pty) Ltd, 24 Sturdee Avenue,
Rosebank, Johannesburg 2196, South Africa

Penguin Books Ltd, Registered Offices: 80 Strand, London WC2R 0RL, England

First paperback edition 2010
Copyright © 2009 by Lynn and Randy Gaston

Most Avery books are available at special quantity discounts for bulk purchase for sales
promotions, premiums, fund-raising, and educational needs. Special books or book
excerpts also can be created to fit specific needs. For details, write
Penguin Group (USA) Inc. Special Markets, 375 Hudson Street, New York, NY 10014.

The Library of Congress has catalogued the hardcover edition as follows:

Gaston, Lynn.
Three times the love : finding answers and hope for our triplets with autism / Lynn and Randy Gaston.
p.   cm.
ISBN 978-1-58333-350-1
1. Autistic children—Care.   2. Triplets.   3. Gaston, Lynn.   4. Gaston, Randy.   5. Parents of autistic
children—Maryland—Biography.   I. Gaston, Randy.   II. Title.
RJ506.A9G397   2009   2008054500
618.92'85882—dc22

ISBN 978-1-58333-379-2 (paperback edition)

Printed in the United States of America
1 3 5 7 9 10 8 6 4 2

BOOK DESIGN BY NICOLE LAROCHE

Neither the publisher nor the authors are engaged in rendering professional advice or services to the individual
reader. The ideas, procedures, and suggestions contained in this book are not intended as a substitute for consulting
with your physician. All matters regarding your health require medical supervision. Neither the authors nor the
publisher shall be liable or responsible for any loss or damage allegedly arising from any information or suggestion
in this book.

While the authors have made every effort to provide accurate telephone numbers and Internet addresses at the time
of publication, neither the publisher nor the authors assume any responsibility for errors, or for changes that occur
after publication. Further, the publisher does not have any control over and does not assume any responsibility for
author or third-party websites or their content.

To our three amazing and handsome sons, Zachary, Hunter, and Nicholas.
Every day you inspire us beyond words, as you face challenges
to communicate in a spoken world.

We love you,
Mom and Dad

CONTENTS

PART TWO. NOT A ROAD MAP BUT A PATH

APPENDICES

FOREWORD

There is no rest for a parent of a child with autism. Each day finds families struggling with the balancing act of schedules and preferences—a favorite shirt that has to be worn every day, an exact brand of peanut butter that must be served at lunch. A child who has these wants and needs, but is struck silent by autism, has no way to communicate them—and even the slightest misstep is enough to knock a family off-kilter. For Randy and Lynn Gaston, parents of three sons with autism spectrum disorders, the struggle is three times as difficult.

We first met the Gastons when they came to us looking for answers two years ago. Our doctors diagnosed their sons, triplets Zachary, Hunter, and Nicholas, with autism. The diagnosis is not easy news for anyone to hear, but Randy and Lynn handled it gracefully. Rather than succumb to fear, they became determined. Not only do they manage to balance the day-to-day challenges, they are able to draw from within and see a larger picture through the fog of autism.

No one needs to tell the doctors, researchers, or therapists here at Kennedy Krieger about that struggle. We have seen firsthand how autism spectrum disorders—brain-based developmental disabilities that affect a child's ability to communicate, understand language, play, and relate to others—can affect families. When autism was first described in the 1940s, it was considered rare, but now 1 in every 150 children will develop the disorder.

Though we still know very little about what causes autism, day by day we are slowly unraveling this mystery. In recent years, we have seen researchers find a handful of genetic markers, begin the search for environmental clues, and test intervention techniques. Because our work has shown that through early intervention we have the best hope of changing a child's developmental trajectory, we are working to lower the typical age of diagnosis from three years to fourteen months.

We are well aware of the toll that autism takes on a family's life, and we are constantly looking for answers to the many questions surrounding this puzzling disorder. Although the path ahead is a long one filled with many obstacles, this is an exciting time for the field of autism because some of the brightest scientific minds are leading our search.

When we began early planning of the first national autism registry, www.IANproject.org—an innovative online initiative designed to accelerate the pace of autism research—Randy and Lynn were among the first in line to offer their support. They took time out of their lives to test the software and help develop questions to better understand the experiences of the families caring for children with autism. Their advice was invaluable, as they truly are experts on autism: They live with it each and every day times three.

Thanks to the efforts of the Gastons and others like them, in April 2007 we launched the IAN Project, which made it possible for parents to provide researchers with critically needed information on autism from the comfort of their homes. The IAN Project also matches families across the country with research studies in their area. This dynamic exchange between families and researchers could lead to new discoveries about causes, diagnoses, treatments, and a possible cure.

When the IAN Project reached its first anniversary, Randy and Lynn were there again, dedicating countless hours to helping us develop a public service announcement that would spread the word about the project and get new families involved. The support of parents like Randy and Lynn is critical to moving forward the work that we do here at the institute.

Randy and Lynn are advocates in the truest sense of the word, and we at Kennedy Krieger have been honored to work with them in raising awareness of and searching for answers to autism. They have become a voice for autism, sharing their story with the world. They are truly courageous and an inspiration to other families.

EACH DAY MAY BE a high-wire act for Randy and Lynn, but they also know that each day with Zachary, Hunter, and Nicholas is

PREFACE

Imagine that out of the blue, your two-year-old fails to respond when you call his name and instead focuses on a plane that's flying thirty thousand feet overhead. Imagine that he suddenly stops speaking, as if a faucet of words has been shut off at some internal valve. Imagine that he begins to avoid your eye, walks away from your hug, and heads to sit in a corner instead.

Imagine entering a room and finding him licking the wall or lining up his toys in a strict geometry only he can fathom. Imagine him walking by his siblings as if he's never seen them before, flapping his arms as if he wants to fly away or twirling around in circles for so long that it makes you dizzy to watch him. Imagine him suddenly developing exotic and arcane preferences and tastes—that instead of chocolate, he turns to eating mulch, leaves, and chips of paint.

Imagine after years of visiting doctors for these puzzling symptoms, a name is finally given to this syndrome—autism—

a life-altering disorder that changes the arc of your family's future and reorders your expectations for his life.

Imagine that this disorder has no proven cure or cause, yet it causes developmental regression and delays in the use of language and social development.

Imagine that you are told that early intervention is crucial for his future, yet no single intervention treatment is guaranteed to work.

Imagine the pressure, doubt, and anxiety as you slog your way through the array of possible interventions. What if you aren't choosing the correct option? How would you know?

Imagine sitting over your bank statements, trying to figure out how to shoulder the financial burden of these treatments—twenty to sixty hours a week, totaling up to $70,000 per year, per child— because your health insurance will not pay for them. And imagine that no school in your area will offer you the best education possible—but only one the schools deem "free and appropriate."

Imagine doing all this while the clock is ticking, while you are watching your child regress before your eyes.

Imagine the realization that while you are holding down a job and caring for your other children, you will need to be an advocate for your child—a full-time job of import and gravity.

If you can imagine all this, you would be imagining our lives, times three. We are the parents of triplet sons, each of whom exhibits a different place on the autism spectrum.

This is our story.

• • •

THREE FACES OF AUTISM:
A DAY IN THE LIFE

Nicholas wakes us up at two a.m. and gestures that he wants to get up.

"Come on, honey," I whisper. "Lie here with Mommy a little bit longer." But no; he's up and nothing can dissuade him. He doesn't convey this in words. Since he stopped speaking as a toddler, he shows us what he means through sign language—strong, eloquent gestures of his arms and hands. He can't tell us how he feels, but he can show us. When he was recently ill with a stomach blockage, he took our hands and placed them over his belly with an anguished look. This was clear enough, though we dream of hearing words.

As I start to get up, he heads into the kitchen; he comes back with a box of Ritz crackers in the shape of various dinosaurs, sits down, and systematically picks through the entire box until he finds the stegosauruses—the only ones he will eat. Then he turns to Randy's computer manual and begins paging through it, one of his favorite activities. It has left the pages dog-eared and moist. He's not really looking at the pages, but something about this activity seems to soothe him—he can do it for hours.

But not today. After a few moments, he looks at me and gestures that he wants to watch a *Sesame Street* video, one he loves so much that he often kisses the screen and sways to and fro when he hears his favorite song.

His activity wakes his brother, Hunter, who also rises and begins toe-walking across the room to his computer to begin one of his games. Toe-walking and stimming—self-stimulating behavior involving twirling, turning, and twisting objects—are the main manifestations of his autism. Like Linus in *Peanuts*, he drags behind him a blue blanket, which acts as a pacifier and helps him remain calm.

Hunter speaks only occasionally and often won't respond to his own name, as if he isn't entirely certain what "Hunter" means. When he walks into the other room, he begins emitting a high-pitched scream—unnerving since it seems to emerge for no known reason.

Our third son, Zachary, is now awake and begins his day by climbing out of bed and searching for his Dr. Seuss books, which he recently has begun reading aloud to anyone who will listen. Our most verbal and high-functioning child, Zachary speaks in snippets and occasionally engages us in meaningful conversation. For a few months now, he's been letting us know when he feels sick by announcing, "Head broke," meaning his head hurts, or even, "I need ice," when he thinks he has been injured. He can't describe the pain, but at least he can give us the location of where it hurts.

"How are you today, Zachary?" I ask him, and he repeats, "How are you today, Zachary?"

His skills of repetition are uncanny. He is unable to say "Hi, Mom," but he can repeat an entire TV show, word for word. He also speaks of himself in the third person. If he sees a photograph and we ask, "Who's that?" he says, "That's Zachary."

We have one son on each end of the autism spectrum and one in the middle. In terms of language and relatedness, Zachary is the highest functioning, Hunter is intermediate, and Nicholas has no language. But they are all progressing.

Randy and I lie in bed a few moments longer, looking at each other in mutual weariness as our boys begin the day on their own complex, private paths. We've slept only three hours, but that is going to be it. Randy has a long commute and a full workday ahead of him; it's a school day for the boys, and a full schedule of important therapies. That means I'll have to maneuver all three through breakfast, dressing, and into the minivan without major meltdowns or crises.

The boys require major assistance getting dressed for school—not their favorite activity. It can be a challenge chasing after them once we get on a sock or shoe. Zachary voices his displeasure by shouting out, "No school!" as he runs from us, so we usually dress him last. We often persuade him to go by telling him that Dr. Seuss also attends school in the same building. When this isn't effective, we say, "It's the law—you have to go," though that doesn't work as well.

Sometimes we wonder why he's so fervently opposed to going to school. Did something happen to him the previous day? Was someone mean to him? But he can't tell us. Our boys are locked in a world all their own, and our days are devoted to breaking through, drawing them out to join us.

I head to the refrigerator and grab a Diet Coke with caffeine while Randy makes coffee. In various rooms, I hear the ping of a computer game, Big Bird singing on *Sesame Street*, and *Green Eggs and Ham* being read aloud by Zachary. It is two-fifteen in the morning, and thus begins another day.

THIS IS NOT SIMPLY our life but that of thousands of families across the country who find themselves consumed by the deep love and immense commitment that are part of raising children with autism.

We had never even heard of the disorder before the birth of our sons, and then we suddenly found ourselves raising three boys with autism. It was difficult enough to have them correctly diagnosed, but even afterward it was hard to find any information on the condition. The Centers for Disease Control and Prevention has been collecting data only since 2001—and that was the year our sons were born.

Autism can place an immense strain on families, who have to reorient their expectations for their child's future while becoming advocates on everything from education to effective therapies.

We have seen the weary faces of parents who struggle with their disabled children, emptying their retirement savings, fashioning their own treatment plans between full days of work and never enough sleep. We understand what it's like, because we have been involved in this struggle ourselves for seven years.

Had we known what we know now, we might not have been stymied by a medical establishment that insisted our sons were normal, by school systems that were baffled and unwilling to accommodate children with special needs, by the morass of treatments, advice, and dead ends.

As we researched and struggled year after year, we also discovered a desire to raise autism awareness, to reach out and advocate for other families so they'd know they weren't alone. The thought of other parents coming behind us and hitting the same wall of indifference and confusion sickened us. At least our struggles might benefit more than our family. And so we decided to write this book, to give other parents the benefit of our experience.

As we continue to work our way through the tunnel toward the light, our boys have taught us so much about courage, persistence, and spirit. They have reminded us why we wanted a family in the first place. It is here that we can offer solace, support, and unconditional love when the outside world is threatening and confusing.

As parents of special-needs children, there are a number of things we can't afford to do—to become ill, to take a day off, or most important, to become discouraged.

Since each case of autism is unique, it's impossible to create a cohesive plan that every family should follow. But through our years of intense research and trial and error, we have come up with a map of our own—including our experience with treatments, educational strategies, and financial realities—that we hope can assist other families as they embark on their own journeys.

We fought hard to bring our sons into the world, and now we are fighting just as hard to help them—and other families like ours—make their way through the difficult but sometimes awe-inspiring terrain of autism.

PART ONE

• • •

OUR STORY

• • •

FLICKERING HEARTBEATS

Randy and I were introduced to our babies the same way as many modern parents—on a sonogram screen in a darkened doctor's office. But because my pregnancy was in vitro, we were able to view them during the first weeks after conception.

At first we couldn't see much on the screen except for a blur, as if a microscope were zooming in and out on an image. But as our eyes became adjusted, we began to make out flickers of light, pulsing like stars against an evening sky.

The doctor said, "Okay, those little flickers are heartbeats."

Then he turned up the volume so we could hear them—the *thump* and *whoosh* of life.

"We're looking for more than one here," he said—our first real verification that we were in fact having twins. "Okay, let's count."

"One flicker," the doctor said.

"Two flickers," said Randy.

Suddenly the doctor's voice fell flat. "Three flickers."

"Triplets!" Randy whooped, in his exuberant touchdown voice.

The doctor told us that our two implanted embryos had split into three; and that two were sharing the same sac, separated by a membrane, a plus for their development.

Triplets! Talk about an embarrassment of riches. In the dark room the images became clearer as a full view of the womb came into focus. Here were the babies—free-floating transparent little tadpoles—so many experts had warned we might never have. It was amazing to see all three of them, spinning and moving freely like acrobats, all attached by their lifeline—the umbilical cord—to me.

I was sustaining life; it had finally happened. Life split into before and after—we had finally stepped into the realm of parenthood.

I felt different already, as if some great switch had been flipped on inside me. I thought of the paintings of the Virgin Mary I'd stared at during Mass when I was little—the look on Mary's face as she gazed down at her infant, as if she were lit by some inner light. I felt that way too, suffused with a kind of ecstasy.

I WASN'T ONE of those girls who always knew she wanted to be a mother, who toted around other people's babies or played quietly under the picnic table with dolls that wet or cried. I was too active for that—a tomboy who preferred tap dancing or climbing trees.

I was drawn to children in a general way—that's why I went to college to become a preschool teacher, and spent hours playing with my nieces. But it wasn't until I met my husband, Randy, that the desire to have a child of my own opened up in me, a chamber of longing I hadn't known before.

Randy and I got engaged late in our twenties. All the customs and traditions that followed—the gold rings, the white wedding, family faces blurred together as they lined the church steps—were a great unfurling of the life that I had begun envisioning for us. In the strength of Randy's devotion, I saw my future and a child standing in the midst of it who would be the embodiment of our love.

We believed that becoming pregnant would be as easy as throwing open a window and allowing a fresh breeze into the room. But as our married life progressed, as one year turned into two then three, conception continued to elude us. I attended baby showers and christenings, kissed the cheeks of dozens of newborns, but they were never ours. As we exited our twenties and entered our thirties, we wrapped our bodies around each other with a growing sense of urgency. Time was marching by and with it our chances. Finally we accepted the reality that we needed help in order to conceive.

Our initiation into the world of fertility was unnerving for both of us—opening up life's most private negotiations to the scrutiny of doctors and bright lights. The Catholic girl in me felt that it was unseemly to mix science with the sacredness of conception. But this girl was being swiftly replaced by another persona I scarcely recognized—a woman in her thirties with a ferocious case of mother love.

As we wandered from one fertility clinic to another, our hopes were regularly dashed. I tried not to resent the pregnant mothers I saw everywhere now, who seemed plump, smug, and serene.

Why was it so hard for us? Randy and I were best friends, hard-working, middle-class people who'd come from a long tradition of family life, and our simple dream was to continue it. We had the four-bedroom house, we had the savings, and now we were waiting for our child to complete us.

We had never imagined that it would be this hard, that it would be seven long years before we received the much-anticipated call.

IT WAS an October afternoon, and we were home together in our Maryland house.

Randy recognized the caller ID of our doctor immediately and called out to me: "Lynn, it's the doctor. Do you want to pick up?"

I raced into the room from the kitchen, a towel still in my hand.

By then I was an old trooper in the fertility world of hope and loss. For years, doctors had been telling us that my chances for conceiving were small, and that the success rate for our latest procedure, in vitro implantation, was even lower.

Yet somewhere inside, I didn't believe it. I couldn't accept that I was actually barren—that awful word that reminded me of a desert, arid and inhospitable to life. Because of my belief that there was a child in our future, I'd allowed the landscape of my body to be probed and prodded, and scanned. My reproductive life had been turned into a science experiment and my body the lab. At that moment, my ovaries were swollen and painful, my belly and thighs dotted with red puncture wounds from the latest round of hormone injections.

I'd endured grueling stretches of these fertility treatments, procedures that were embarrassing when they weren't downright comical. One day when I found myself in line to drop off a vial of Randy's semen, I hardly knew how to reply when the young receptionist asked innocently: "How can I help you?"

Where should I start?

Yet as I stood in our kitchen that autumn day, I was still hopeful. "You answer it," I said to Randy.

The doctor told Randy to put me on the other line so we both could hear the good news. Time seemed to slow as I walked across the room with my damp tea towel—this, I knew, might be our last chance.

"We've got a pregnancy!" the doctor said, as if this were a team effort, which of course it was. What hadn't we tried to become pregnant? It was all a haze now—the blood drawing, the cold metal examining tables, the stirrups and injections.

The latest, in vitro, had been the most harrowing: First, birth control pills to regulate my cycle, then fertility drugs to stimulate the ovaries, so that I would produce as many eggs as possible.

Then retrieval of the eggs, which were injected with sperm while we waited in the lab, reading tattered copies of *People* and *Sports Illustrated* while the doctor determined which of the fertilized zygotes were most likely to survive.

Finally, the most viable of these zygotes were implanted into my uterus. We have photos of these cell clusters the day they were implanted; to anyone else they would have looked like amoebas from a high school biology book, but to us, they were beautiful. We looked deep into them and tried to discern the possible profile of a daughter or son.

Now, on two different extensions, Randy and I both burst into tears at the doctor's words of success.

He went on with some caveats: I was going to have an uphill battle; my hormone levels were extremely high, almost quadruple the normal value of a typical pregnancy, which suggested, at the least, twins. But twins sounded great to us, and nothing could drown out the roar of our happiness.

RANDY AND I were thrilled that day we saw the first sonogram of our babies, but something was wrong with the doctor. His whole demeanor had changed. He had moved away from us and looked sullen and disappointed.

"I wish this hadn't happened," he said.

What was he talking about? The heartbeats were healthy and strong.

"What's wrong?" Randy asked him.

"Triplets are high-risk pregnancies. We don't consider them a success. We'll have to monitor you continually to ensure that all goes well. In the meantime, I want you to consider the possibility of reduction."

Reduction?

That was another of those medical terms—*products of conception* was another—that we'd heard plenty of during our fertility odyssey. *Reduction* meant allowing one of the embryos to die in an attempt to increase the chances for the others.

I gazed at Randy with one of those long, silent looks of marriage. We didn't even need to discuss this, but the doctor insisted we take a moment by ourselves.

"How could we ever choose which one dies?" Randy asked.

I shook my head—this would never be possible for either of us.

We had worked long and hard to have these children, whoever they might be in the future.

"I'll need a lot of help with them, you know," I told him.

Randy put his arm around me. "I'll make sure you have all the help you need."

It turned out that we didn't have the slightest idea how much help we would need or what lay ahead of us in the uncharted future, but Randy's words were—and still are—good enough for me.

I MUST HAVE HAD one of the most monitored pregnancies in history—weekly ultrasounds, continued injections, extensive tests to make certain the babies—who we'd learned were all three boys—didn't have Down syndrome or other birth defects.

For me, there was no such thing as morning sickness, but an all-day nausea that blanketed me every waking moment. Like a pregnant wife in a comedy, I craved a particular food—chicken teriyaki, for example—and by the time Randy returned home with it, the sight and smell made me so nauseated that I'd send him out for another whim, veal Parmesan.

I swiftly gained fifty pounds, the recommended weight gain for triplets. But the amount of strain this placed on my back was enormous. I felt like a beast of burden, yoked with a tremendous load. The bigger I grew, the harder it was to breathe or sleep. I caught my massive reflection in shop windows and was stopped by the sheer novelty of being happily and fruitfully fat. I knew my weight gain meant the babies were thriving, and any discomfort was a validation of my precious cargo.

In my new maternity outfits, happily purchased online, I was in a golden haze. Finally, we could let down our guard and allow ourselves to dream. I lay on my left side, like a beached whale, and watched Randy paint the nursery blue and decorate it with Winnie-the-Pooh accents, then arrange three beautiful oak cribs, gifts from my family.

Toward the end of the pregnancy, at twenty-seven weeks, I was placed on complete bed rest after experiencing preterm labor pains. I was permitted to get up only to go to the bathroom. Before Randy left for work each day he prepared a day's worth of meals and placed them in a mini refrigerator by the bed. There I remained, inert, day after day, monitoring the boys' inner gymnastics—a knee here, a foot there. Their activity thrilled me. Day by day, they were headed toward us and our lives together.

2

• • •

AND THEN WE WERE FIVE

Despite our months of planning, the night I began labor Randy was as nonplussed as if I had been expecting for nine days instead of nearly eight months. I sat up on the side of the bed and shook him awake around eleven o'clock on Saturday, June 2.

"What?" he muttered.

"Wake up," I said. "I think my water just broke."

He rolled over and looked at me skeptically. "Are you sure?"

I pointed at the stream of water that was slowly trickling down my leg to the floor. That did it—I could see his mind flitting back to the birth lectures we'd attended: *Water breaking, amniotic fluid, first stages of labor.* In other words, the boys' births were imminent. I'd carried them almost to my due date—thirty-five weeks, which is considered a success for triplets.

Randy bolted out of bed as if he'd been struck by lightning, and began frantically tearing through the house. First stop was the kitchen, where I heard him dialing from a list of numbers that were posted on the refrigerator.

My bag mostly packed, I moved gingerly around the bedroom, as bands of pain began wrapping around my abdomen then making their retreat. This wasn't so bad, I told myself, as I began timing my contractions. I felt a wave of exhilaration; the birth of the boys, so long anticipated, was beginning at last.

I lumbered downstairs and met Randy at the door. He had only been able to reach our doctor's answering service and was beside himself that the doctor hadn't called back yet.

"It's the middle of the night—she'll call," I reassured him, but I had worries of my own. The boys weren't scheduled for delivery via C-section until Wednesday. What if the hospital was booked up like a hotel and unable to accommodate us?

Randy packed the car, and soon we were barreling down Route 97 so fast that I was sure we'd get a speeding ticket. I guess we were both pretty nervous; when his cell phone rang, we both practically jumped out of our skins. It was our ob-gyn, saying she was already on duty at the hospital, waiting for us.

At least we could relax about that. But meanwhile, I had changed my mind about the contractions; my earlier pains were being swiftly replaced by a deeper, more wrenching variety. I braced myself in the car seat as they swept over me. *You can take this,* I kept telling myself. I focused on the fact that a day from now, this would all be over, and these fierce little souls who were beginning their exodus from my body would be out in the light of the world, in our arms. I had to remind myself of this many more times that night as the pain notched up to ever more intense levels.

Once at the hospital, we were shuttled up to the labor and

delivery floor. The boys were to be born in a birthing pavilion where natural childbirth was encouraged—but not for me, not that night. I was hooked up to fetal monitors and given a cascade of medications to prevent various complications and to place my labor on hold.

It turned out that June 2 was a busy evening, with many babies queued up to enter the world. Like a plane circling the airport, I had to wait my turn since there were several expectant mothers waiting ahead of me.

During the hours of suspended animation, while the boys were waiting to be born, we were treated to a concerto of their heartbeats, an echoing, reverberating medley as the chambers of their hearts pulsed open then closed.

Hang in there, I told them, wrapping my arms over my stomach. I was frankly enormous. It was a feat of nature that my abdomen had been able to stretch enough to encompass my vast circumference.

By now, the word *excruciating*—a term I'd never had the misfortune to consider before—had begun to enter my mind. Each new pain opened up into one deeper and more long lasting. I remembered overhearing female relatives claiming that they couldn't remember the pain of labor once it was over, but I couldn't imagine how this could be so.

Randy slipped out to call my mother, who appeared soon after with my sister at her side, both of their dear faces radiating love and concern.

"You're going to be fine," my mother murmured, and I reminded myself with a jolt that she should know. She'd been through childbirth herself, four times.

Finally it was our turn, and we entered the cold and sterile-smelling OR.

"I love you," Randy said, as he stood flanking my left side, while the anesthesiologist stood on my right.

"I like you too," I said, recalling an old joke from when we first dated.

I had already received an epidural and would remain conscious throughout. My numb lower body was draped like a private stage so I couldn't see the actual C-section being performed. I didn't need to see it—I was well aware of the process. The doctor would be making two horizontal incisions, one through my abdominal wall, and another into my uterus, where the babies were. In order to control bleeding, he would be using a special knife that cauterized the tissues.

I may not have been able to see, but I could feel the tugs and make out the doctor's exertions as he worked to extract the boys. Behind Randy's mask, I could see his eyes alter, brighten, and finally fog with tears as we heard the first wail of life. From 4:59 to 5:03 that morning the boys were born, each weighing four pounds. One after another, the cries continued as they were lifted from my body, then raised in the air, as if in blessing.

Both Randy and I had lost our fathers the year before we met and married. We often spoke of our regret that they wouldn't be present to witness the birth of their grandsons. Yet when the doctors raised the boys high for us to see, I felt that all of our families, past and present, were united in their homecoming. We had already picked the boys' names ahead of time, incorporating the names of our fathers. For reasons of simplicity, the hospital labeled them Baby A, B, and C. But they were Zachary Leonard, Hunter Randall, and Nicholas John to us.

Even though Hunter and Nicholas were identical twins, they were visibly different from the start. Hunter was longer-legged, and Nicholas had a far rounder face. Both were tiny as birds, their eyes closed and their faces smeared with Vaseline. Randy cut the umbilical cords, and the room filled with their scalding cries.

We anxiously checked their pink and crinkled bodies, counting that everything was intact—six little arms, legs, eyes.

From the first hour of our sons' lives, we got a taste of the deep curiosity engendered by triplets. Everyone who worked in the unit wanted to have a peek at them and ask the kind of questions that we would become accustomed to over the years.

"Are those real live triplets?"

"Wow, that must have been painful!"

And our favorite, "Are they all *yours*?"

Oh, yes, I thought, lying exhausted and half numb. They were ours, all right.

I WAS HANDED Zachary to hold while Nicholas and Hunter were whisked away for weight and measurement checks. Or so I was told. In truth, they were being frantically transferred to the neonatal intensive care unit because they were having difficulty breathing on their own.

Soon enough, the anesthesia began to wear off and my pain returned, accompanied by a whiff of alarm. Where were the other boys? And why was Randy roaming back and forth between intensive care and my room? Why was he giving evasive answers when I asked, "What's happening with Nicholas and Hunter? Why can't I see them?"

And there was this: I knew my mother's face as well as my own, and something had happened to the unadulterated joy I had seen there earlier.

I was still unable to walk, but the nurses finally agreed to wheel my gurney into the NICU to check on Nicholas and Hunter. I felt a jolt of panic when I saw a group of nurses milling around them. Each boy was in an isolette or clear glass crib, a tiny biosphere for premature infants that simulates a warm germ-free environment. These little terrariums were where our boys would live for the next few weeks.

Hunter was taken out of his isolette and handed to me, as light as a leaf, his eyes still tightly shut.

I stroked his hairline. "Hi, Hunter," I said, and he slowly cracked open his left eyelid and peered up at me like a little sparrow and let out a cry. It was almost as if he were winking at me, saying, "Don't worry, Ma, I just need a little time to get adjusted."

I was thrilled that he had responded to my voice; I had been crooning to him all these months. I gave him back reluctantly, and turned to Nicholas, watching helplessly as a cluster of nurses fussed over him.

He was struggling, thin and yellowed from jaundice, under a bili-light. He had been blindfolded and had had a tube placed down his throat to aid his breathing. His desperate attempts to cry were stymied by the tube.

Now I understood why Randy was so frantic and my mother's face suddenly so tense.

"You can't hold him," the nurses kept telling me when I tried to reach out for him. But how else would the poor little guy, blind to the world, know I was there?

The best I could do was touch his hand through the opening in the isolette. His fingers flexed and extended at the contact.

THE NORTHERN CORNER of NICU became triplet central for the next long weeks, an enclave of our relatives as our boys struggled to stabilize.

During those days and nights of hope and worry, I gained a new regard for the nurses who tended to us, who stole in on their soft-soled shoes, who patted our hands and dispensed something far more precious than medications. Sometimes in the half-light, they seemed like angels, hovering over our children, so raw, new, and exposed.

"Time's on your side. This is the best place Nicholas can be now," an older nurse told Randy during those rough days when our baby's condition remained uncertain. These words were priceless to us, and we would remember the comfort of them later, during other hard times.

As Nicholas's breathing slowly began to improve, he proved himself to be a little fighter. Even though he couldn't see us for several days, we rubbed his back, sang, and spoke to him. One afternoon, when he wrapped his tiny hand completely around Randy's index finger, we knew he was going to survive.

After several weeks the boys had gained weight and were strong enough to be released, one by one. Nicholas, surprisingly, went home first, followed by Hunter and finally Zachary.

Then the afternoon arrived when Randy shut the front door of our house behind him and gave me a long hug. Lined up in their tiny bassinettes, the boys watched their relieved, exhausted parents take in the enormity of their new lives, surrounded by a mountain of disposable diapers, toys, and baby equipment. Five of us where there had once been two. Home together at last.

We'd gotten through the hard part, and now there would be only smooth sailing.

That's where we were wrong.

3

• • •

THREE TIMES THE LOVE

My brother's wife had given birth to twins two years before, so they had a head start on the challenges of newborn multiples. My brother made us a spreadsheet so we could keep track of feeding, diaper changing, and naps for each boy.

Based on his experience, my brother stressed that a strict schedule was essential. He warned that if the boys didn't sleep and eat around the same time, we would disintegrate into chaos—a sleepless, bleary household of bawling infants, dirty diapers, and unsterilized bottles.

I saw immediately what he meant. As preemies the boys needed to be fed every two hours around the clock. They were ravenous, drinking four color-coded bottles of special formula. Their formula was expensive—over twenty dollars a day—but luckily Randy had a wonderful career that also enabled me to stay home with the boys full-time.

I found it difficult to sleep during the day, thus disregarding a cardinal rule for triplet mothers: You should always nap whenever your babies do. And since the boys mixed up their days and nights and tended to be fully active at three a.m. instead of three p.m., Randy and I weren't getting much sleep. I found myself groggily placing the formula in the freezer and the laundry in the oven, among other strange acts.

From the moment the boys were born, I developed an acute second sense. I knew each boy's distinctive cry as well as what it signified—Zach's hunger sounded different to me from Hunter's wet diaper. I was hypervigilant, aware of the boys' every burp and whimper. I was always checking on them, making sure they were lying in their bassinettes on their backs, always checking their little chests to see if they were breathing properly. I was keenly aware that they were preemies who were still supposed to be in the protection of my womb, not out in the germy, dangerous world.

Maybe that's why I was so fiercely protective. When a neighborhood teenager wanted to come over to visit, I made certain she washed her hands before she entered their room, and then hovered beside her.

"They're like tiny dolls," she exclaimed, bending over to peek at them, and something in her innocent delight reminded me of myself when I was young.

IT WAS SUCH an immense relief to have the boys home. There was no time to think, just to do what needed to be done. I was on some strange kind of overdrive—when I wasn't washing bottles, I was sterilizing nipples or doing laundry. I learned how to prop the boys up on a pillow and feed them bottles, fit all three on my lap, sleep under only a thin layer of unconsciousness. These and other parental skills I developed by some strange osmosis.

Any newborn is challenging, but handling three was a massive undertaking, requiring complex maneuvering and foresight. We adopted an assembly-line approach to many chores, laying out three sets of clothes, assembling three bottles, keeping two rocking chairs in constant motion. We were exhausted, but this sweet chaos was part of what we had dreamed of—all the toys and mess, scheduling and clutter were family life.

In between the feeding and burping I spent plenty of time just bonding with them, holding their tiny bodies against me in thanksgiving. During these early months, I gained a new appreciation for my own mother, who had raised four children herself and now was helping me out whenever she had the chance. It was only now, with my new perspective as a harried mother, that I realized all she had contended with in those early years when she had made my own childhood seem so effortlessly peaceful and content.

The boys delighted us, each in his own way: Hunter's winsome smile, Zachary's curiosity, Nicholas's affectionate energy. Sometimes in the evening when they lay in a warm pile around us, I looked over at Randy and saw in his face the glow of contentment.

Still, we were frankly exhausted, especially when the boys fell ill at the same time, going down together like a line of bowling pins. Randy always took off work to accompany me to the doctor, but sometimes we had to schedule appointments later in the day, after he arrived home.

That's what happened one afternoon when the boys were about six months old and all got sick with the same virus. Randy had gotten out of work late, and we found ourselves rushing to our pediatrician's office.

I turned to my sweet husband as he drove and wondered if I looked as tired as he did. One of the drawbacks of having young triplets is that you have no time or energy to focus on anything else; the possibility of a night out together for dinner or a movie had long ago vanished. When we sat down now at the end of the day, we folded laundry or cleared up toys and talked about the boys.

I worried about what a strain it was for Randy to travel such long hours, then rush home whenever the boys had an appointment.

"Maybe you should start looking for work closer to home," I said to him. "If there's an emergency like this, it takes you over an hour to get here."

This was a topic fraught with emotions, since not only was Randy successful at his job, but he provided our family's sole income. As the lead network administrator in his information technology job, he worked long hours and had to remain perpetually on call in case anything went wrong with a client's network. It was a demanding life, made more stressful by our three newborns.

While we discussed the pros and cons, the boys napped in their infant car seats. Not paying attention, Randy was doing thirty-five in a twenty-five-mile-per-hour rural zone lined with horse farms. Out of nowhere, the flashing blue lights of a police car approached. Randy muttered as he pulled over to the side and waited for the officer to come up to the car window.

"Where are you folks heading in such a hurry?" he asked.

I chimed in before Randy could reply: "Sorry if we were speeding. We're on the way to the doctor. Our babies are sick."

"Babies?"

He stepped back and peeked into the rear window to see the boys asleep in their car seats, nestled like three peas in a pod, blissfully unaware of our drama.

Something about triplets seems to make people distrust the proof of their own eyes.

He asked, "Are they triplets?" and his tough policeman demeanor vanished, replaced by a look of tenderness.

Randy nodded. "Yeah, they're just six months old."

The policeman said, "Well, you have more on your plate than I do. Have a nice day, and slow down!"

As we pulled away Randy looked at me in disbelief. "He didn't even ask to see my license."

"He was a dad—I could tell," I said.

Plus, I guess we must have both looked pretty tired.

AFTER OUR LONG fertility quest and prenatal saga, we'd assumed that we were through with doctors for a while. We'd had enough of nurse's stations, beeping monitors, and needles for the rest of our lives. But soon after their first birthdays, all three of them required eye muscle surgery when their eyes turned inward and crossed.

They also developed a condition called torticollis from being crowded in the womb. This neck condition made them unable to turn their heads side-to-side all the way and required physical therapy three times a week. We hired a wonderful private physical therapist who found a way to perform physical therapy with each boy as if he were simply playing with them.

During this period we also visited a pediatric urologist to find

out what to do about Hunter's birth defect: a urethra with an ab-
normally placed urinary opening. The doctor suggested that it
would be best for Hunter to have the surgery to correct this as soon
as possible.

Around this time we also noticed that Nicholas had begun a
constant inconsolable weeping—all the more upsetting since he
couldn't tell us what was wrong

"He's just teething," the pediatrician told me when I took him
to the office, but I knew it had to be more than that. I took him
back five more times before the doctor finally concurred that Nicholas was not teething, but instead needed emergency surgery to
repair an inguinal hernia—a protrusion of abdominal cavity con-
tents through the inguinal canal. Just as I'd feared, he'd been crying
out of pain.

It had been deeply ingrained in me, the obedient middle daughter of a Catholic family, to be the peacemaker, especially in the face
of authority figures such as doctors. The hernia incident began the
slow dismantling of the passive girl in me, who held her tongue and
meekly followed any physician's pronouncement. It was also a painful foreshadowing of future encounters with officials, medical and
otherwise, who downplayed or discounted the boys' symptoms.

I vowed that if Nicholas ever cried like that again, I would re-
fuse to disregard it until all medical issues had been investigated.
But at that time, I would have never believed the fierce advocate
I'd eventually become.

I FOUND IT wrenching to be back in the hospital again with both
boys, and even harder to watch them being prepped and whisked

off to surgery, dressed in their little gowns. One parent was allowed to stay with each boy in the OR until he was given anesthesia, but I just couldn't go into the operating room. I found it nearly unbearable to hand them off this way—to a room of strangers where I couldn't monitor and keep them safe. The alternative was nearly as painful—sitting for hours in the waiting area, imagining the action in an operating room floors away.

Randy bravely stayed with each of the boys as they were wheeled into the OR and kissed them on the forehead before he was asked to leave.

His drawn face was testament to what this cost him—but that's how he was, always wanting the boys to know he was there with them even in the scariest of times.

Both boys quickly recuperated from their surgeries, but it was a challenge to handle Hunter's catheter bag, which he had to wear for several days post-surgery. How do you tell an eleven-month-old that a bag protruding from his body isn't a toy to be played with or tugged out? Not so easy; we ended up clothing him in one-piece outfits that fit over the catheter and were able to keep him occupied so he wouldn't fuss with the tube.

During that first year of assorted illnesses, Nicholas also had eleven ear infections and was prescribed eleven separate antibiotics. It seemed as soon as one infection went away, another returned. During this period, Hunter's eardrum also burst; the doctor had no idea why. Later I would discover that many children with autism suffer from frequent ear infections, but at this point I was blithely unaware of such issues, and the word *autism* was still as foreign as *inguinal hernias* and *torticollis* had been the year before.

• • •

FOR THE BOYS' first birthday we had a big bash, featuring cake, and party favors based on *Bear in the Big Blue House,* a favorite TV show of the boys starring a gentle bear who's joined by other forest creatures as he teaches concepts like sharing.

All three boys were growing apace and reaching milestones typical for their age. We sat amid our relatives and watched as the boys sat, crawled, and walked holding onto the furniture, and we happily spun scenarios about their futures.

"Zach could be a pitcher—look at those arms," someone remarked. "Maybe Hunter'll be a doctor, the way he studies things."

That's how we were then, trying on different futures for our boys as if they were overcoats.

We had decided early on to document their lives by taking weekly digital photos. The ones from this birthday highlighted the boys' sunny dispositions, which were out in full force: Nicholas's laughter as he made a mess with his blue birthday cake, Hunter's smiles as he bounced inside his ExerSaucer with his cousins, Zachary's hugs and kisses.

Those photos are particularly poignant to us now—the boys' faces so vibrant and happy, something in Randy and me still so naive and young. Looking back, I realize that this was the best time of our lives, before the storm clouds began to gather, before the daunting word *autism* entered our lives.

Randy and I seemed to be always on the go, maneuvering the boys in their triplet strollers and cutting a wide swath through malls, family get-togethers, and parks, attracting even more scrutiny and curious questions. *Are they twins?* became our new favorite, inexplicable question.

The boys kept me constantly on my toes. My attempts to keep track of them bordered on slapstick, especially in the backyard, where they would split into three separate arcs of activity. I thought that my feinting, rushing, and fancy footwork would hold me in good stead when I became a football, soccer, or hockey mom, as I fully intended. These boys had the energy and perseverance to fuel a team or two.

IT WAS GOOD we were still young; when I saw parents in their forties and fifties with twins or triplets, I couldn't imagine how they did it. Still, I hadn't known that it was possible to be so tired—sometimes at the end of the day, every part of me ached, from my toes to my teeth. But the physical exhaustion was mixed with so much happiness.

We had no clue that in another couple of months our happy world would be rocked.

4

• • •

ESCALATING MELTDOWNS
AND ODD BEHAVIOR

When the boys reached a year and a half, their pediatrician suggested that they receive their required eighteen-month vaccinations. Like other newborns, they'd already received their first vaccinations for hepatitis B on their second day of life. Even though they were only four pounds at the time, they were vaccinated as typical infants, with no adjustments for their weight or their five-week prematurity. Was the threat of hepatitis B so pressing that it required this early, massive vaccination? We didn't even think to ask. It was simply standard operating procedure, one of thousands of medical protocols that we did not particularly note or question.

We were shocked, however, when we saw the list of thirty-some vaccines that the boys were due to have before the age of six and the number of them that were to be given at the eighteen-month juncture. This was more than double the ten that Randy and I'd had as babies. I could understand the meningitis and whooping cough, but why did the boys need a chicken pox vaccination? It was a fairly minor illness that Randy and I had both missed only a week of school over.

Was it really necessary to have so many of these vaccinations all at once? This was current medical practice, the doctors told us, part of an attempt to prevent children from acquiring an increasing number of infectious diseases.

Well, we were all for that; we believed in vaccinations and knew that they had saved thousands from deadly illnesses such as polio. Besides, who were we to question doctors, who assured us that these vaccinations were not only necessary but safe? Modern medicine had saved our boys as preemies and improved their lives during their first year of life. As usual, our desire was to do the absolute best for them. And so we acted, as we had before and as we have since, on our children's behalf, based on current thinking.

Like most people, we entrusted the fates of our loved ones to a medical establishment we'd been taught to honor and respect. Later, we realized that this establishment was not a single monolithic force that had all the answers. We also came to realize the vaccination debate had many players, as well as many layers of complexity.

While we believe in vaccinations as a lifesaving force, if we could go back and do it again, we would have spaced them out instead of having so many, so early, and all at once. For there is no arguing with the fact that in the six months following their eighteen-month vaccinations, our boys began to regress right before our eyes.

Before *my* eyes, I should say. Randy still could not bear to see it.

• • •

SINCE THE BOYS were preemies, I had always been concerned about their development, measuring them against other babies I encountered. A common preoccupation of new mothers.

"Ginny is in the top first percentile in weight and the top third in height," a neighbor announced proudly one day when we encountered her on a walk. I looked at Ginny with a competitive eye, then rushed back home to chart the boys' percentages online.

They seemed to be hitting most of their developmental milestones. They were gaining weight and height, eating well and on target for eighteen months—taking us by the hand and leading us to the refrigerator when they wanted a drink, for example. With their tawny hair and bright eyes, they were the picture of health and vitality. We doted on their every advancement.

Their speech was somewhat delayed, but since they were not only premature but also boys and triplets, this didn't seem out of the ordinary.

Then, as if some internal clock had simultaneously gone off in each boy, our sons began to develop odd new behaviors.

Nicholas, who had been speaking a few basic words, went completely silent one afternoon. "What's wrong, honey?" I asked him. "Can't you say 'Mama'? How about 'Daddy'?" But no; suddenly he couldn't, and no other sound emerged from his mouth again unless he was laughing or crying.

Instead of cuddling up with us as he usually did, he gravitated off by himself, sitting alone, staring out the window. He began to play inappropriately with toys; he wouldn't hold a train or car upright, but would turn it upside down and regard it from all angles. He began staring, seemingly mesmerized, at lights.

During this same period, Hunter began to arch his heel upward and glide across the floor on his tiptoes, as if listening to some ballet music only he could hear. He started to lick odd items—the couch, a pillow, his shoe. He picked up any wheeled toy and spun the tires over and over. If I tried to turn the toy right side up, he became upset. At night, he roamed the house emitting a high-pitched scream.

And then, to my disbelief, Zachary began his own changes. He became compulsive, lining up his cereal boxes and toys. The first time he lined up his Thomas the Tank Engine train cars in single file, I thought he was doing this because it was the pattern that trains usually traveled. But then he started lining up his blocks the same way, and everything else in the house. If I moved even one of them out of alignment, a ferocious tantrum ensued.

He covered his ears when there was a loud or unusual sound. And he couldn't tolerate change in his routine. If I put on the wrong cartoon or gave him the wrong book or shoe, he became so upset that there was no calming him.

EACH DAY, I watched the boys change before my eyes. It was almost as if someone had turned a switch off; as if, developmentally, their first eighteen months had never happened.

I also noted a change in the way the boys appeared in our digital photos. There was now a certain distance—often they didn't look directly into the camera anymore but off at some obscure point on the horizon.

What was going on? I was dumbfounded and terrified and in dread of what I might find when I opened my eyes each new day.

Randy commuted long distances, then worked long hours, only to return to an exhausted wife who was desperate to chronicle her worries.

"Look at the way Hunter's walking. And Zachary shouldn't be crying like that."

But by the time he got home at seven p.m., the boys were winding down from the day, and their symptoms were much less acute.

After all our long struggles, he could not allow himself to consider that anything could possibly be wrong. He wanted to hug them, take off his shoes, and eat his dinner.

"They're fine," he said, trying to comfort me.

That's what my friends and family said as well.

"They're only two—wait and see. Lots of two-year-olds act this way. Especially boys. Especially preemies, and triplets."

But in the middle of the night I had become a secret detective, trolling the Internet, stuck for hours on sites that linked symptoms with disorders.

I plugged in "toe-walking," "withdrawing," "tantrums," and the same word kept popping up: *autism,* a chronic neurological condition that affects communication, social, and self-help skills and has no clear cure or cause. It didn't matter how many other symptoms I added or in what order, that odious term continued to appear like a taunt, chilling my blood.

I discovered that there were four distinctive symptoms that characterize autism: a delay in language, and difficulty with communication; lack of social interaction and development; a need for sameness, coupled with repetitive or obsessive behaviors; and un-usual reactions to sensory stimuli. These behaviors can be as mild as avoiding eye contact or as severe as complete withdrawal into a private world. Among my three sons, I saw them all.

I found that there were terms for many of the behaviors I'd been observing for so long. Every child's autism manifests itself in various forms, and two of the most common were stimming and echolalia. Stimming occurs when a child continuously ratchets, twirls, or spins an object repeatedly, gaining some sensory gratification in the repeated motion. Echolalia is the act of repeating speech, mimicking the speaker's words. I learned that some children with autism may never speak and it's unknown why this happens.

I learned that these characteristics can vary greatly in severity. No two children are alike. With a sinking heart I realized our sons seemed to be like links of a necklace on this spectrum—from our nonverbal Nicholas to the high-functioning Zachary, with Hunter in the middle range. But the common denominator among them was an impairment in social relatedness that made it difficult to learn and communicate.

Night after night, I read until I couldn't bear it anymore, then turned off the computer and walked into the living room. It was painful to stand in the doorway, witnessing so many behaviors I'd just read about on the computer.

STILL, SOME PART of me just couldn't believe it. No one in our family had ever suffered from autism. The only example I'd ever *heard* of was the character Dustin Hoffman played in the movie *Rain Man.* That wasn't our boys.

And how could we possibly have three?

I started to doubt my own judgment and powers of perception. Maybe I was exaggerating these changes, a function of staying home all day, with only the company of toddlers.

To make things even more stressful, our formerly healthy toddlers began falling ill with every virus they encountered, experiencing prolonged episodes of unexplained vomiting and high fevers. We had to rush Zachary to the hospital one night because he was dehydrated from so much vomiting, and the doctors had a difficult time hooking him up to an IV so he could receive intravenous fluids.

Meanwhile, our house became the site of escalating meltdowns that Randy and I struggled to understand: A change in waffle brand, a rainstorm, a wrong turn on a car trip—all could cause inconsolable weeping from the boys, each of whom had his own unique triggers.

Going on outings to the doctor or to visit family were massive undertakings, fraught with pitfalls we could not foresee. What would set the boys off, and how could we comfort them? We couldn't possibly fill our van with the contingency items required to ward off a possible tantrum—the alternative shoes, toys, books, and crackers. There were simply too many variables and triggers.

I wracked my brain about what could have brought this on. The boys had been perfectly healthy. What had changed, what had we done, in the last months? There was nothing, except for their vaccinations. In the end it was easier to stay home and make life as regimented as possible.

I started avoiding the competitive young mothers with their charts and percentiles; I begged off when we were invited out. There was no time for sleep, let alone friends. The boys might go to bed at eight, but at least one of them would be up at two, waking the others.

Exhausted and frazzled, Randy and I begin to bicker. I wanted him to acknowledge the severity of the boys' regression, but he kept finding excuses, saying "They're kids—it's a phase." I was exhausted and terrified and felt I had nowhere to turn. One of the many disturbing facts I'd gleaned online was that the divorce rate in families with children with autism is a staggering eighty percent. I could barely let my mind light on the prospect of myself as a single mom, trying to cope with the boys. I could barely handle things now. I not only loved Randy but also needed him in order to manage the daunting task that had become our daily lives. I added this to my list of escalating worries. There was not just the day to get through, but the future.

The websites were scaring me to death with their cautionary tales of bankrupt families and blasted futures. And something else was worrying me: Every website on autism I found stated that the earlier a child receives intervention, the greater the chance for success. Brain development begins before birth, and there is a tremendous degree of change that occurs in the first five years.

I felt a clock ticking under our lives—what if we were losing precious time? This couldn't wait forever. When the boys didn't keep me sleepless, this knowledge did.

Finally I gathered my courage and took all three boys to their pediatrician for their two-year wellness visit.

I had decided beforehand that I was going to let our son's pediatrician know of my concern that the boys might have autism. From my research, it had become clear that they would need immediate intensive therapy. In order to get this ball rolling, we needed a medical diagnosis.

• • •

5

SEARCHING FOR A DIAGNOSIS

We had always respected our pediatrician, a bright woman who was a mom herself and whose office was lined with a montage of her patients as well as her children. She was also a twin, so we felt that she had a unique understanding of our boys.

She examined each of them with Randy and me assisting. Because the boys were fussy, it was a juggling act to keep them all lined up and occupied. None of them was thrilled to have her peek into his ears or mouth or eyes.

When she finished, she looked at their charts and said: "Well, they look great—their weight is fine. You'll be glad to know that they're all within the normal percentiles for their growth."

I felt a wave of relief. Maybe I could just release this worry like a helium balloon, simply leave the office pretending everything was fine. But for the boys' sake, I couldn't allow myself to harbor such illusions. I had been witness to images no one else had seen, scenes of our boys acting in ways so bizarre, so completely different from anything I'd ever witnessed, that I couldn't keep quiet any longer.

"I know this sounds crazy," I blurted out, "but I think they might all have autism."

Our doctor laughed out loud as if I were making a joke. "They'd be the most socially developed children with autism I've ever seen. You're just worrying. They're fine."

I persisted, presenting a list of all the boys' new behaviors, which sounded ominous even to me. What about toe-walking, loss of eye contact, picky eating, arm-flapping, loss of language for Nicholas, lining up of toys, covering of the ears, meltdowns, and sleep problems?

She listened to me, but I could tell she was unmoved. "All toddlers do these things," she said. "Let's just wait and see. My teenage son had many of these behaviors, and he's fine."

Complicating matters was the fact that the boys had what educational experts called scattered or splintered skills—meaning that their development was all over the place. While Hunter could not say "Hi" or "Bye," he could recite his ABCs—an advanced skill. Zachary could operate a computer, but he didn't know how to ask me for something to drink. Nicholas was cuddly and affectionate but refused to call me Mama anymore.

Still, the pediatrician insisted, this could all be attributed to being preemies and boys.

There was never a point in my life when I so wished to be wrong. Everything in me wanted to throw the burden of my worries out the window. Maybe I *was* simply being an oversensitive mother.

In fact, if I had tried to look from the doctor's point of view, the boys seemed at that moment simply rambunctious triplets, their sunny dispositions far from the withdrawn stereotype often associated with autism.

In her defense, pediatricians were not trained at that point to spot autism at such a young age. In fact, autism wasn't even a part of medical school training. The Centers for Disease Control began collecting data only in 2001. And it wasn't until 2007 that the American Academy of Pediatricians set up new guidelines to assist physicians in diagnosing the early signs of autism, so that children could obtain early treatment.

But our boys were born in 2001, and this was far too late for us.

I was also aware how much Randy ached to be reassured by our doctor, even though it kept us on opposing courses—a lonely route for me. I needed my husband to join forces with me, and he just wasn't ready yet. And now he had an unexpected ally in our pediatrician. Our *former* pediatrician, that is. As much as Randy wanted not to believe my fears, he was as turned off as I was by our doctor's disregard of my worries.

As we left the office with only a referral for an ear, nose, and throat doctor to check the boys' hearing, Hunter did the oddest thing—he licked the doorknob.

But I was the only one who saw him.

• • •

6

CHAOS, FLAPPING, AND SPINNING

If someone had peeked into our living room window, they wouldn't have believed the barely controlled chaos that soon became our lives—a topsy-turvy world where each of our sons moved deep into his own private diversions: Zach whirling in circles, Hunter jumping on his trampoline, Nicholas swaying in front of a computer, his favorite video blaring.

There was so much activity that it was hard to keep track, but that was my job—mom in the middle, trying to anticipate their needs, soothe, and love all at the same time.

The changes in the boys continued, dizzying in their scope and variety.

Hunter began consuming inedible items such as play dough, leaves, and the mulch we placed around flowers. He didn't comprehend the concept of danger. If I let go of his hand when we were outside, he darted immediately into the road even if a car was coming.

When we took him to the park, he was more interested in studying the letters on the "Do Not Trespass" sign than in playing on the swings or on the slides. At the park he also liked to pace, nowhere in particular; he just kept walking. It was great for exercising but unnerving because I couldn't understand why he didn't seem tired after his long walks.

Zachary covered his ears if something bothered him suddenly; it could be a noise, a sound, or sight. If he saw a baby at the doctor's waiting room he covered his ears—as if in anticipation of the baby's crying. He became deeply absorbed in lining up his trains, DVD boxes, anything, according to a strict internal architecture that only he could see. His day had to be highly structured; he had a meltdown if anything was out of place. He would cry and scream if we took a different route when driving to a familiar place. If his clothing became wet or stained he needed to have it immediately changed.

And then the changes grew more bizarre.

Hunter began to flap his arms throughout the day, especially when he grew excited. To a stranger it might have looked as if he were imitating a bird or pretending to be an airplane, but Hunter wasn't imitating anything in particular; he was doing this for no clear reason.

While Hunter was flapping, Zach had begun spinning in circles like a whirling dervish. It made me dizzy just to watch him, but I couldn't get him to stop.

Autism has been described as a disorder of extreme aloneness. In varying degrees, all the boys had the ability to ignore and disregard the outside world, but I saw it particularly in Nicholas.

He had always been so affectionate with us, but now he preferred to spend much of his time alone. He sat in silence, staring out the windows or at the ceiling fan, and wanted to engage with us only on his terms. I couldn't get him to use a spoon or fork. Sometimes he wouldn't respond to his name, even if I screamed it at the top of my lungs.

It seemed each week brought new developments. Zachary grew so distraught one morning when it began raining outside that I could calm him only by closing every mini blind in the house.

I was exhausted and frightened. Some days when they fell asleep for a blessed nap, I sat amid the rubble of toys and cereal bowls and child development books and prayed that someone would help us.

I couldn't face this alone. I needed Randy beside me. At first, when I showed him my research, he searched for rational explanations for each of the boy's symptoms. But beneath his pride and denial, I saw I was slowly breaking through.

One day when he came home from work, I found him standing in the doorway, watching as Hunter licked the kitchen floor, then stood and began systematically licking the wall, then the window sill, then the sliding glass door.

I'd witnessed this behavior many times, but Randy seemed shaken up by it. Later that weekend we were outside with a new swing set that we'd recently assembled. Instead of swinging or sliding, Nicholas darted out toward our tiger lily garden and became transfixed with the lilies. Over and over he tried to pull the bulbs from the stems and eat them.

"Stop, Nicholas," Randy said, trying repeatedly to redirect him toward the swing set. But nothing mattered to Nicholas except the flower bed.

Later, after Randy had prepared his plate for lunch, Zachary had a meltdown, wailing at full force and arching his back as if he were in physical agony.

"What's the matter?" Randy asked.

I looked over. "His sandwich and chips aren't lined up the right way. Plus he doesn't use that red plate—he only likes the white one for lunch."

As I told Randy this, he looked over at me, and I saw in his face that he'd finally accepted that something was seriously amiss with our boys. For me, this was a relief and a heartbreak all at the same time.

Among other things, Randy had imagined a Gaston family football team, with himself the proud coach. This and so many other visions of the boys' futures would have to be readjusted. If my hunch was correct, our boys would not have the carefree childhoods we'd dreamed of, the kind that we'd had ourselves.

Now we just had to find someone to verify what we already knew.

I was terrified. Where should we go? How could we intervene, when I couldn't get anyone to agree with us?

It's not as if a parent knew these things ahead of time. You could open the phone book and find information on diabetes or dialysis, but autism was listed nowhere, as if it simply didn't exist.

KEEPING TRACK of our boys as they regressed was not just physically exhausting but also emotionally overwhelming. Both Randy and I were both now actively researching which treatments might work for them, where we might find them, and how we would pay for them. The problem was that there was no clear direction for us to follow. As a booklet published by the National Academy of Science, "Educating Children with Autism," starkly stated: "There is not a simple, direct relationship between any particular current intervention and 'recovery' from autism."

"How come there's no clearinghouse or guidebook?" Randy kept wondering.

We couldn't believe the lack of definitive data, when there was so much information about so many other disorders and ailments: childhood diabetes, depression, attention deficit disorder, and cancer. Added to this was the specter of the boys' futures—whether they would be able to make friends and eventually grow independent. Surely there were other parents who were going through the same thing, but we didn't know where they were and we were too exhausted and overwhelmed to try to find them.

I came upon Randy many times in the middle of the night, slumped in front of our glowing computer, confronted with lines and paragraphs of conflicting advice. We never forgot the loneliness of those months of solitary searching, just the two of us and the Internet, trying to make sense of the boys' new worlds and our new lives.

IN OUR EFFORT to obtain a definitive diagnosis of the boys' condition, we decided to go to the top and make appointments with the most reputable institutions and doctors we could find.

Having grown up in Maryland, I was aware of the international reputation of Kennedy Krieger, a facility that serves children and adolescents with developmental disabilities, part of the Johns Hopkins medical institutions in Baltimore.

Once I started my research and began talking with parents of children with special needs, the name kept coming up. We called to make an appointment and were given one far in the future.

At the same time, I discovered Dr. Stanley Greenspan on the Internet when I was researching Floortime, the first treatment we began using at home. This technique stressed getting down on the floor at the child's level and playing in that natural environment while following the child's lead. As it turned out, Greenspan was the founder of Floortime, and he resided in Maryland, too.

Given the fact that we had triplets, we thought he might agree to see the boys and offer his opinion. When we contacted his office we were told that he rarely saw children, but that we could be placed on his extremely long waiting list—with the understanding that we might never see him at all. Given his esteemed reputation, we decided to take our chances.

Between Kennedy Krieger and Dr. Greenspan we believed that we would eventually receive the definitive diagnosis that had eluded us elsewhere. The problem was, the waiting time for both of these appointments was likely to stretch over a year.

Even though we still had no official diagnosis, our research had made it clear that the boys might be in serious jeopardy if they didn't receive early intervention. There was a window of time when therapies for the boys' developing brains would be most effective, and I was terrified it would close. We felt that we were playing Beat the Clock.

And so Randy and I redoubled our efforts to figure out which therapies might work for the boys. It was a daunting task; there were so many to choose from. We spent many nights in front of the computer, cruising different educational websites. That's where we learned about applied behavior analysis (ABA), one of the most commonly employed therapies, which is highly regimented and centers on repetition and reward.

We also talked to people in the field. A therapist told me about applied verbal behavior (AVB), which appealed to us because it focuses on communication and language. There was also traditional occupational and speech therapy to consider. Our house was filled with books and printouts, our heads with conflicting advice. But in the end there was no clear way to ascertain which treatment might work best for each boy—other than trial and error.

We hired a young woman named Nicole to work part-time with two of the boys while I worked one-on-one with the other using Floortime, which was designed to help the boys achieve the developmental skills they were missing. This therapy is based on the notion that development consists of a ladder of milestones that children climb, one rung at a time, and in sequence. If a child hasn't mastered a rung-two milestone, he can't move on to a three.

In our boys' developmental ladder, certain rungs were either missing or there had been a regression to an earlier stage. For example, while the boys had taken us by the hand and led us to the refrigerator when they wanted something to eat or drink—an important twelve-to-eighteen-month milestone—they had never advanced to such twenty-four-month milestones as engaging in pretend play.

These milestones were crucial links that most parents don't even consider, involving social interactive skills, a sense of connectedness, or linking emotions to behavior.

While other children were becoming more interactive with others, our boys were heading in the other direction—avoiding eye contact, becoming increasingly immersed in a world of their own. Their brains needed to be engaged in human interaction, and Floortime was a way of accomplishing this.

It also seemed the least invasive of the therapies, and was appealing because it could be spontaneous and fun, allowing us to follow our children's lead. It also could be done in their familiar, natural environment.

This treatment turned out to be effective with all three boys, though Nicole didn't last long; the intensive, one-on-one work was slow and difficult. Working with your own beloved child is one thing, but for a young woman interested in part-time work, this kind of therapy can become extremely tedious. And it was hard to facilitate this program with three children six times a day.

MEANWHILE, the changes in our sons continued. It was during these months that all three of them turned into picky eaters. They went from eating a wide variety of fruits, vegetables, and chicken, to being extremely selective, each boy with his own unique palate. Randy and I often felt like short-order cooks.

Zachary, for example, would eat only waffles for breakfast, and not just *any* waffles. They had to be a certain brand with a particular texture. He would even watch vigilantly as I prepared them to make certain that they came out of the correct package. Other than waffles, he would eat only chicken stew, pizza, applesauce, and crackers. If I tried to offer him something different—carrots or cereal, for example—he would scream or completely refuse to eat.

Nicholas, on the other hand, would eat only pizza, crackers, and chicken nuggets. He also developed an unquenchable thirst for milk, drinking so much of it that I became worried that he would make himself sick. In some cases of autism, a child cannot tolerate casein and it causes hyperactivity or irritability.

Hunter would eat only waffles, graham crackers, chicken nuggets, applesauce, and frozen pizza—each of a particular brand. If I took any of these items out of the wrong box, he would simply hand them back to me in silent refusal. Occasionally I kept the boxes around and found a way to get him to accept items by taking them out of his approved packaging, but it wasn't easy to fool him.

To complicate matters, Hunter and Nicholas would eat only Celeste brand frozen pizza. They knew the shape and the design of the box and the location of it in the freezer. It had to come out of that box in order for them to accept it. Zachary's pizza, on the other hand, had to be fresh from the local pizzeria, thick-crusted with a sweet tomato sauce.

The boys were deeply vigilant about these preferences—almost as if their lives depended on them. These weren't behavior problems in the sense that they simply wanted to have their way. The boys would rather not eat at all than go against their deep predetermined desires.

It was as if I were feeding three little connoisseurs of strict and unvarying tastes who would not swerve from their choices. I was worried that they weren't getting enough fruits and green vegetables.

All the boys also developed acid reflux at this time. The doctor prescribed Zantac for them all, and when that didn't help much, she prescribed Prevacid. They also began having bouts of loose stools—watery, with a foul smell, unlike anything I'd ever encountered before.

But when I spoke to the pediatrician about these problems, she told me simply to add vitamins to the boys' diets and that these were common toddler issues. Once again, I felt dismissed and unheard.

THERE'S AN IMAGE from the boys' second Christmas that remains in my mind: Nicholas, sitting apart from his brothers and cousins, studying his hands as if they were a fascinating new development, something he'd never seen before.

"Wow, Nicholas must love his hands," one of his cousins remarked, and I made light of it, but inside I felt like crying.

This was a new behavior—and signified to me that he was continuing his backward retreat from us. His hand-staring wasn't a sign of self-esteem or admiration but one of his growing autistic symptoms.

Christmas at my mother's had always been a family tradition.

She had a flair for making this holiday beautifully special—the trees, the packages, everything shiny and perfect. Only now with three rambunctious boys I saw it all in a new, nerve-wracking light. What had once been a gorgeous holiday display now was a collision course full of breakables, inedibles, dangerous corners, and harrowing stairways. And I couldn't help viewing all this from my sons' perspective—a disturbing assemblage of strangers coupled with brightly lit trees just waiting to be touched, packages beckoning to be torn open, mounds of food ready to be sampled.

Randy and I spent Christmas Day lurching from room to room, chasing the boys, forestalling innumerable disasters. Somehow in public, the boys' regression appeared even more painfully glaring.

Hunter was so overstimulated that he paced the rooms like the Energizer bunny, never sitting down for more than a moment before beginning his new rounds. Nicholas kept trying to eat the beautiful red and white poinsettias arrayed throughout the house; the fact that they were poisonous made his attempts even more unnerving. Zachary became so overwhelmed that he broke down in one of the most massive tantrums we'd ever witnessed, wailing and crying. There was nothing we could do to calm him except to leave.

The boys' first Christmas had been spent at our house, and had been exhausting but a success. However, much had changed in the last year, and if I had needed a sign of just how much, this holiday was a sore reminder. I realized later that this Christmas was a turning point. Some part of me had simply wanted the boys to have time with our extended family, for our relatives to know and love them as much as we did and share their lives. But this day showed me that I had to face certain facts, and one of them was that

• • •

7

MAKING THE WORLD SAFE
FOR OUR BOYS

It was a cold day in January 2004, and the boys, two and a half years old at the time, were napping. They hadn't been sleeping well, and I was exhausted myself from being up with them most nights.

The circles under my eyes had circles under them. I brushed my hair and dressed each morning barely glancing at myself in the mirror. This was one of many things there was no time for.

We were in the middle of the limbo years, still without a diagnosis, working with the boys one-on-one on the basis of our own exhaustive research and frantic devices. We were their advocates, their bridge to a world that seemed to be shrinking ever smaller.

Our daily life had become an unending push to locate services that would help our boys during these crucial early years. By then we had trundled them to speech therapists and hearing specialists, and had availed ourselves of limited services from the school system's infant and toddler services—a deflating experience. Many of their therapists didn't show up or even call to say they weren't coming. And when they arrived, they seemed more interested in chatting among themselves than working with the boys. In the end we privately hired our own Floortime therapist, occupational therapist, and a young woman to work part-time one-on-one with the boys. We knew our sons needed more than this, but in the meantime we had no choice but to continue our Floortime work and wait for the medical appointments that seemed ages away.

That January day I'd decided to warm up the house by putting a few logs in the wood stove on the lower level—an old cast-iron model with a spring-loaded temperature gauge that clicked as the temperature rose.

I had lit this stove many times, and had the procedure down pat: I placed a bunch of kindling under the X that I'd created, so that there was ample air to fuel the fire.

The boys' bedroom was on the main level, so as soon as I got the fire going, I headed back up to check on them in their crib tents, a recent and welcome addition to their rooms. Cozy and snug, these tents seemed to provide them a safe shelter, and the boys seemed to love the cocooned feeling of being tucked into them.

As I reached the landing, the cordless phone rang—Randy, calling from his car.

"I'm just heading home. How'd the day go?"

Just as I began to answer I noticed a white haze of smoke floating up from the bottom floor, then the downstairs smoke detectors went off in a synchronized wail.

Without saying a word I dropped the phone, leaving Randy to wonder what was happening, and dashed back downstairs to find that the wood stove had come open and a fire was spreading quickly across the carpeted basement floor. Flames had already engulfed the curtains on our sliding glass doors. For the first time in all the years we had used this stove, the door had opened and a smoldering ember from a burning log had shot across the room, igniting the blaze. But I didn't know that at the time. I was aware of only the fiery curtains before my eyes.

I was astounded at how rapidly a fire could ignite and spread. In my panic, I was momentarily frozen, as if mired in cement. I realized in the same moment that there was no way that I was going to be able to put out this fire myself. And how would I ever be able to get all three boys out at the same time?

I rushed upstairs into the boys' bedroom, where Nicholas and Hunter were still sleeping but Zachary was starting to wake up. The fire on the floor below was almost directly beneath the children's beds. By this time Randy had surmised what was going on from the wail of the fire detectors. He had called the next-door neighbors, still with a good hour drive ahead of him.

For my part, I realized that I had to call 911. I got on the line with a dispatcher and gave her my address and explained my situation. As I talked, thicker smoke started snaking its way up the stairs, and I realized I had to hurry.

"Please stay on the line," the dispatcher said.

"I can't—I need both arms," I said, dropping the phone.

I unzipped the crib tents and took Zachary and Hunter out. Out the window I noticed two teenage girls walking home from school, as if from a tableau of some earlier, carefree life. I rushed to the window and screamed out, *"Fire! Help!"* The girls looked up and then dashed over. I flew down the stairs, carrying both boys under my arms like two logs, opened the front door, and handed them over.

By now I could hear fire engines in the distance, and smoke was pouring out the front door. I covered my mouth with my shirt and flew back up the stairs to Nicholas. I unzipped him from his crib tent, covered him, and ran with him in my arms down the stairs and out of the house to the neighbor's house where Zachary and Hunter had been taken.

Apart from the massive disorientation of being woken by smoke and a terrified mother, the boys seemed dazed but fine. I turned from them to the window. From next door, the view of our burning house was surreal, like watching a movie. The fire was extensive now. As far as I knew, we might lose everything. It was that thought that propelled me to wrap the shirt back over my face and head back in a second time, my neighbor Sandy joining me.

Why was I so adamant about going back inside? Over the last years, since the boys had begun regressing, Randy and I had desperately constructed a cache of toys, clothes, and other familiar items that helped comfort them.

Routine had become the law for us; without it, chaos ensued. Every detail of our daily life had to be carefully plotted with an eye for sameness and ritual. The sheets on the boys' beds had to be the same; we had to drive the identical route whenever we went to the store, and bathe them each night at the same hour.

Any unexpected change was extremely upsetting and induced an unpredictable reaction. A familiar toy or blanket was imbued with meaning and comfort that was hard to convey. If the boys had massive tantrums over my switching waffle brands, I could just imagine their reaction to being uprooted by a terrifying fire from their orderly lives and cocoonlike beds. For our sons, who thrived on sameness, this was potentially a disaster.

That was why I found myself with my shirt over my face, frantically plunging through our closets, grabbing as much as I could before the smoke rose further. It was the middle of winter, and I needed warm clothes for the boys, along with their favorite cuddle toys that helped make them feel secure.

My neighbor kept saying, "Lynn, we'd better go. We've got to go!" and finally I turned away. Smoke was everywhere now, and we ran out just as the fire department arrived—two fire trucks and a police car.

The firemen began making their way through our house, trying to extinguish the fire as quickly as possible. Moments later, paramedics rushed over to our neighbor's to make sure that the boys and I were fine. Our neighbors opened their home to us while we waited for Randy to arrive home, breathless and anxious from his hourlong drive.

When the fire was finally out, the firemen came over and delivered the verdict: The fire had destroyed part of the lower level of the house; soot blanketed everything, and the house was uninhabitable until it was glove cleaned, item by item.

We may have lost insulation, carpet, ceilings, computer, toys, and TVs, but we were under no illusions. We had been extremely lucky—we were all alive and well, and that was what mattered.

My mother was away on vacation and offered her house to us while our house was cleaned. But after a single night chasing the boys through her beautiful rooms, filled with knickknacks and crystal, we decided it was better to go to a local hotel to rent a suite that had a kitchen, living room, and two bedrooms.

For the boys' sake we tried to make this hotel suite a fun mini vacation for them, setting up as many games and diversions as we could. But without the comfort and safety of their everyday routine, let alone their cribs, they were disconsolate and remained sleepless the entire week we were away from home—which meant the same state for Randy and me.

The fire made me realize how vulnerable we were, tied to a routine that could be upended at any moment, sending us into chaos and confusion. The seven days it took to clean the house seemed like an eternity.

8

PRESCHOOL AND THE
POLITICS OF AUTISM

What was most memorable about the boys' third birthday was that they didn't realize it *was* their birthday. They knew they were receiving gifts and were happy with the cake and the attention, but the significance of the day was lost on them.

It was hard to explain how painful and frustrating it was to watch the boys continue to regress by some invisible process that we were unable to stop, cure, or even find anyone to name. It was not comparable to any other condition. Had they suffered damage from a birth defect or accident, they would have been swiftly assessed by the medical establishment and treatments prescribed and paid for by our insurance company.

But as it was, we simply watched in desperation as they slipped erratically backward or off into new territories we'd never witnessed before.

Time was marching on, and they were falling more behind than ever as we waited for our appointments with Dr. Greenspan and the Kennedy Krieger Institute.

We decided to move ahead in one of the few areas where we had some control: getting the boys into preschool so that they could begin to receive early intervention services. We had no choice but to investigate public preschools, since I'd already learned that the boys' developmental issues precluded them from entering a private one. The first step was to take them to Child Find, a component of the Individuals with Disabilities Education Act (IDEA), which requires states to locate and evaluate all children with disabilities who are in need of early intervention. We were placed on a long waiting list for this service, but finally our February appointment arrived. On our long journey of delays and misdiagnoses, these meetings would prove to be the most fateful.

The boys were set to be evaluated at a local public school that was now used for special-needs children from ages three to twenty-one. I had my first pang when we pulled up to the building—a drab, neglected brick structure that looked as if it hadn't been maintained for years. I couldn't help thinking that whatever went on inside these walls couldn't have been highly valued by the powers that governed this building.

We met with the Child Find team, consisting of a special educator (whom I'll call Sally), a school psychologist, and a speech-language pathologist, or SLP. It was immediately clear that the special educator ran the show.

The team decided to split us up, with Sally going off to evaluate Hunter and Nicholas in the school gymnasium while Zachary and Randy met with the SLP in a separate room. I was no expert, but I was acutely aware that trying to evaluate both Hunter and Nicholas at the same time—and in an ancient gymnasium—was not a great idea. But this was part of the protocol to get the boys into preschool so I held my tongue.

Once in the gym, Hunter and Nicholas tore off like shots on their separate paths—Hunter opened the equipment closets and took out balls and bats, while Nicholas began climbing on the parallel bars and other equipment meant for older students. Sally dashed between them, trying to corral them together for an evaluation but it was fruitless. The whole process was hard for me to watch. Then Nicholas had one of his tantrums, and Sally realized her folly at bringing them here. She asked that we reschedule.

Meanwhile, the SLP was meeting with Zachary, who was demonstrating his echolalia by echoing and mimicking her words. While the SLP told Randy that this might indicate autism, she decided to label him as developmentally delayed instead, a far less serious diagnosis that would also garner him far less treatment.

Nicholas and Hunter were rescheduled for evaluation on a cold overcast day in March. We traveled to a nearby playground, where they were placed in baby swings, and Sally observed them for fifteen minutes as they swung silently back and forth. I watched their little faces, bundled in hoods, against the gray sky. Of course, they had no notion that they were being assessed, or that their futures might hang in the balance. But the truth was that as a result of this short interlude, Sally labeled our boys mentally retarded, or MR— a devastating misdiagnosis that would be as long-lasting as indelible ink, and almost as impossible to remove.

She did not provide the boys with standardized testing. There was no speech-language specialist to evaluate their speech or school psychologist to talk at length with us and with the boys. There was no special educator to look at their previous development, or occupational therapist for a sensory evaluation. The boys' fine motor skills, social awareness, receptive and expressive language, gross motor skills, and adaptive behaviors were not assessed. All these steps, which are required before this serious and life-changing diagnosis could be made, were omitted. Instead our boys were simply watched as they silently swung back and forth. They didn't speak, so they were labeled MR.

Later, when we were sadly wiser, we learned that it was the policy of the Maryland county where we lived then that a formal autism diagnosis should *never* be rendered until a child was age five—which meant missing the entire early intervention period.

We also discovered that an MR diagnosis costs a school system far less in services than a diagnosis of autism, especially when it affects triplets like ours. Autism therapies are expensive, as we would continually personally learn.

Randy and I were flabbergasted by the diagnoses. Our boys had been completely normal for the first eighteen months of their lives, so we were absolutely certain that they were not MR. But the evaluators urged us not to worry about this label, which they claimed could be easily deleted, and was being used simply as a means of classification in order for our sons to receive services.

But in fact this serious misdiagnosis was an egregious violation of our children's educational rights. And all it availed us was the most miserly of services—and only twelve and a half hours of preschool along with fifteen minutes of speech therapy per week the next autumn.

It was our misfortune at that time to reside in an antiquated county whose evaluative methods were still in the dark ages and which still held the misconception that children with autism *are* mentally retarded. This was our harrowing introduction to the bureaucratic delays and missteps that we became sadly familiar with over the next fateful years.

By now we were certain of what our boys were suffering from, but no one else would yet agree with us. The disregard and blindness of these professionals reminded us of how Zachary covered his eyes when he was confronted with something that was too upsetting for him to look at or process.

OUR NEXT PEDIATRICIAN was an improvement over the previous one, but he was still uncomfortable giving the boys an autism diagnosis. He said that he would leave that up to Dr. Greenspan or people at the Kennedy Krieger Institute, whom we were still waiting to see.

Obviously the word *autism* was to be avoided at all costs. But it was this specific label that we knew held the key to the extensive services our sons needed and deserved. We knew from our research that a child with autism could learn—given a suitable environment and appropriate teaching methods.

On one doctor's visit, the pediatrician made Randy furious when he made the offhand remark that our sons would never be baseball players.

"How does he know the boys' futures?" Randy railed on the way home. "They're only four years old! Nobody should shortchange them or write them off that way."

We realized that we would have to raise the level of our advocacy to new heights. It was up to us—we were the boys' one link to the world.

We spent even more hours researching new therapies, diets, and programs—anything we thought might benefit the boys in even the slightest way.

Randy and I began discussing how to get them more services than the local Child Find team provided. We had to confront the facts that stared us in the face every morning: If we didn't provide speech therapy, the boys' language skills would not progress further. Nicholas would remain silent, and Zachary would continue to repeat what others said. Without occupational therapy, Hunter might never use a fork or spoon, drink from a cup, or draw a straight line.

Along with Floortime, which helped the boys connect on their age level and gain the social and emotional skills they needed, we decided to begin applied behavior analysis (ABA) and applied verbal behavior (AVB) to help them work on speech and academic skills. These therapies were essential in order for our boys to develop into functional children in tune with their peers.

We were already trying to turn every daily activity into its own tiny therapy session: Playing trains became a pop quiz, and asking for a drink a chance to reinforce verbal skills.

Spurring us on were the glimpses that Randy and I continued to get of how our sons would be without autism. Sometimes, it was as if a gear had slipped and they were back for a moment, the way they were before their regressions.

All at once, Nicholas occasionally appeared to understand what we were saying to him. He would give us a look straight in the eye, and a deep smile that seemed a glimpse into his soul and his potential. He also had a little ironic laugh that seemed to say, Ha-ha, I really get it, and you guys don't realize how much I really understand.

This also happened occasionally with Hunter. In the middle of tickling him, he would stop laughing and say something intimate, clear as a bell.

And there was the memorable moment when Zachary returned home from school one day and sauntered into the kitchen and said, "Hi, Mom, how are you?" as if he were a typical young boy without a care in the world.

These portals into their world gave us a renewed determination and strengthened our marital bond. I felt we were finally on the right track together, even if we couldn't seem to find anyone in the medical community who shared our enthusiasm or optimism.

The financial costs of the prolonged therapies our sons needed were staggering and not funded by our health insurance. Hourly rates were as high as $100 per hour per child. We were looking at up to $70,000 per child times three. We began brainstorming on how to raise money, but we had few real options. Randy couldn't work any harder than he already did, and I couldn't go back to work since there was so much I needed to do for the boys.

What did we have? Our house, in a high market. Perhaps we could take a home equity loan, or even sell our home and move to a neighboring county that had more appropriate services for children with autism.

We'd learned that there was no federal autism policy and that states differed in the services they offered. Maryland was one of a handful of states that provided Medicaid funding for autism, but the waiting lists for services were so long that our children could age out of them while waiting.

Autism was affecting an increasing number of children—1 in every 166 children at the time—and they would all need services, which would weigh heavily on school budgets. Much depended on how a particular county valued education and how well tax dollars that fund it ultimately trickled down to classroom services.

Still, the thought of moving, on top of everything else, was almost too much to bear.

• • •

9

HOPE, DETERMINATION—
AND A PLAN

The bleak and overcrowded atmosphere of the preschool the boys were scheduled to attend had remained in my mind. So it was with a heavy heart—and against my better judgment—that I began driving the five miles to take them there in August. At the moment, this uninspiring location was our only option.

Because of their lack of communication skills, I was reluctant to let the boys ride the bus, even though getting all of them dressed, fed, and in the van each morning was a massive, time-consuming operation.

I had a general terror of the boys' being taken advantage of, given their lack of suspicion or sense of danger. Hunter, in particular, was so trusting that I was afraid that any stranger who showed him interest could simply lead him away.

From the moment I walked into the school that first day, I had a bad feeling in the pit of my stomach. The secretary in the main office was as grim as a prison matron, and I sensed again that this wasn't the place where our sons were going to find the education they deserved.

The school turned out to be a United Nations of disabilities and special needs: children with cerebral palsy, Down syndrome, speech delays, autism, and global developmental delay. Each of these disorders posed distinct challenges and deserved discrete and unique forms of therapy, but they were all crowded together here.

The teachers were to be using a type of structured learning called TEACHH with our boys, but I could see that they were overburdened with the multiple challenges of their students and didn't know where to begin.

Even though we were thirty miles apart, Randy and I spent our days simultaneously worrying whether the boys were safe, whether the teachers really understood autism, and whether the other children were bullying them. The thought of their being taken advantage of or being mistreated kept us in a state of apprehension.

Since school lasted only a little less than three hours, our van became my mini home; I was always on the verge of taking them or picking them up. But even when I was home, it seemed a teacher was always calling, complaining that one of the boys was upset—his notebook had been torn or his shirt was stained—and couldn't be calmed and couldn't I please come back and pick him up?

Once when I returned to school after such a call, Zachary's teacher said to me, "I don't understand why he's crying so much and taking up all my time. He's only developmentally delayed."

"He's not developmentally delayed, he has autism," I told her.

"That's not what it says here," she insisted, looking at what was written on his Individual Education Program (IEP) forms.

"I don't care what it says. I know what my son has."

But it was useless, like arguing with a brick wall.

Still, the boys attended school sufficient hours to catch every virus that was circulating that season; there was a two-month stretch that winter when our house became a veritable sick ward of cross-communicated illness, all of us ill and vomiting with viruses that we kept passing back and forth to each other.

It wasn't simply that the boys were becoming ill and making little progress in this preschool, but when we picked them up, we found that they were unfed and had spent most of their day napping. They were also marked with ballpoint ink initials to differentiate them from each other, as if they were sports equipment.

And then there were the desolate looks we saw on other parents' faces as their children were herded together in what was more a babysitting setting than a learning environment. One afternoon, I walked beside several mothers who gave off such an air of exhausted hopelessness that it broke my heart.

"They say she has autism, but I'm not even sure what that means," I heard one mother tell another about the silent towheaded daughter she was picking up. "I've got three more at home, and my husband's lost his job. This is all I can do."

I couldn't get this girl or her mother out of my mind, and I talked about it with Randy one night. "It's like she's given up on her daughter already, and she's only five."

Despite everything we may have lost—our savings, our home, and sometimes, it felt, our minds—we hadn't lost our hope and determination. But we knew exactly how hard it was to gather together the scattered information and find appropriate treatment for autism.

"Maybe we could find a way to bring together experts in one place so more parents could learn what was available," I said to Randy. But I was really thinking that maybe we could find a way to show people that if we could do it with a little support, they could too.

Randy looked around our chaotic rooms with a half-smile—a shoe was on the living room table, and the kitchen was still a mess from our Friday-night pizza dinner. I knew him so well that I could almost hear what he was thinking. *When exactly would we find time to plan something like this?*

But I knew something else about my husband: If he had an ounce of energy left, he would spend it to advocate for our boys and others with their plight.

At night after the boys went to sleep, we began talking about how we might facilitate the kind of event that would help other parents avoid our own arduous search—gathering doctors, therapists, and organizations in one spot on one day to explain all the available options they had to choose from without spending their life savings—a kind of synergistic educational banquet. We looked on the Internet and found another organization in Ohio that was planning a similar event. We shared ideas and listened to their valuable advice.

We knew we'd need volunteers and a keynote speaker with stature. During our rare spare moments, we began making calls. We weren't even certain that there'd be interest, but we quickly found that there was. Physicians, attorneys, and therapists agreed to help families navigate this complex world. Respected organizations, such as the National Institutes of Health, Kennedy Krieger Institute, and Duke University, were eager to participate. We found space at a local community college, and Randy purchased a domain name and began building the site.

And thus our Autism Expo took on a life all its own.

IN THE MEANTIME, to deal with our own frustrations, Randy and I widened our circle of specialists, consulting special-education attorneys and consultants who were familiar with special-education programs. One consultant told us that we should consider moving to neighboring Howard County, where the boys would be offered more appropriate services. We paid her more than $1,100 in fees to tell us to move to a neighboring county; we told her we'd consider it.

Then came the January morning when I walked into the house after dropping off the boys and received another phone call from the school. This time it was the nurse, and my heart dropped at her words.

Nicholas had been injured and would be returning home with a blackened right eye.

"What happened?" I asked, horrified.

No one was exactly sure, but she reported that the consensus was that he had run into a bookshelf—an unlikely scenario. What it really meant was that no one had been watching our silent, vulnerable boy.

When I called Randy and told him about the incident, I could feel his outrage seeping through the phone. He arrived home early, and we drove to school in a burning silence, both of us occupied with our fears and worries.

How were we going to protect the boys, while ensuring that

they were getting the intensive, specialized treatment they needed—all without a diagnosis?

We met with the teacher, the principal, the vice-principal. They were suitably apologetic, but nothing they said could rid us of the sense that the boys were languishing in this preschool, something they—and we—couldn't afford.

On the way back home, Randy looked over at me and said, "We're going to have to sell the house and move to a better school system. It's the only way."

I had somehow believed that our house, the boys' cocoon and our haven, was sacrosanct, the one thing I couldn't part with. But as I took my husband's hand in silent agreement, I realized that I'd been wrong.

• • •

10

A DEFINITIVE SECOND OPINION

When Randy and I looked behind us now, our path was littered with so many deferred dreams, and a private Catholic school education was only one of them.

That didn't mean we were sad or regretful; we didn't feel sorry for ourselves. We might have had little time alone for dinners out or evenings with friends. Our world might have been smaller than we liked, but that didn't mean we were unhappy. We treasured our boys and refused to give up on them. We saw them as full of enormous potential, and our foremost goal was to make certain it was nourished.

While moving would be a huge upheaval, it was the only way they were going to get the services they needed and deserved. Howard County, where we decided to relocate, had a fine reputation for providing services to children with autism. The county also had Maryland's highest percentage of students with autism disorders. Randy and I had lived there when we were first married, so we were familiar with the area. But the truth was, we would have moved to the moon in order to find help for the boys.

We found a real estate agent to list the house, signed the listing agreement, and made a leap of faith.

AFTER SO MANY MONTHS and years of waiting, events began to accelerate and happen all at once. Our house sold within a week, hurtling us into a frenzy of packing, planning, and house-hunting. We'd moved into our house as a newlywed couple and now were exiting as a family of five. The combined accumulation of our lives was monumental—books, clothes, and toys—but we dove in head-first. Nothing was going to stop us now.

It took us two months to find a suitable home in Howard County, which we decided to rent rather than buy in case the new school system didn't work out. We were able to slowly acclimate the boys to our new home by bringing them over on weekends and letting them wander around the new rooms.

They were able to finish the rest of their preschool year in the new county, where they were immediately availed of occupational therapy and speech therapy—an hour a week instead of the miserly fifteen minutes they had previously been given.

In fact, the new school system proved to be light years beyond our previous county in terms of autism awareness, with a tremendous understanding of the kind of intensive, perpetuating, and consistent intervention our sons needed. The move was a big upheaval, but we were grateful and relieved that we'd taken the plunge.

• • •

By a twist of fate, after waiting more than a year, the two critical diagnostic appointments occurred within a few weeks of each other, and just after our move to the new school district.

Our Kennedy Krieger appointment was first, held in Baltimore at the Center for Autism and Related Disorders surrounded by a famous Baltimore icon, TV Hill.

Once we were finished with the intake process, we were taken to a tiny back office that was small for one child, let alone three. Yet our boys found plenty to occupy them, including a collection of wooden giraffes lying on the desk. The developmental pediatrician and respected neurologist Dr. James Rubenstein entered this cramped space and closed the door behind him. Well coiffed and wearing a blue Armani suit, he looked more like a celebrity than an expert in the early identification of children with autism. After a quick handshake he ushered yet another person into this cramped space, a neurologist colleague who, he explained, would be performing the main observational portion of the exam.

After a few moments, Dr. Rubenstein excused himself, and the neurologist went over our family histories while the boys milled around, picking up every object that wasn't nailed down.

Once she had completed her questioning, she observed the boys playing in the cramped space. They displayed many of their common behaviors—stimming, staring, toe-walking, Nicholas off by himself in silence. Afterward, brandishing little hammers and lights, she gave them each a brief physical exam. By the time she excused herself and left to confer with Dr. Rubenstein, Randy and I were feeling mighty claustrophobic.

We looked over at each other as she shut the door behind her. We weren't sure what we expected, but was this it?

Even though we knew from our research that there was no scan or blood test that could detect autism, it was still a shock to realize that our boys' long-awaited diagnosis was almost completely reliant on visual screening.

When Dr. Rubenstein reentered, he looked solemn and far less chipper. I studied his face as he sat down and finally uttered the words that we had been anticipating: "Mr. and Mrs. Gaston, all three of your boys have autism."

I looked over and saw a flush of color wash over Randy's face. Here was the confirmation that we had been awaiting for so long; I had been seeking validation of my instincts for years now, and I knew that this diagnosis was key to obtaining services the boys desperately needed.

Yet the sound of those actual words made something inside me collapse. Suspecting a diagnosis is different from hearing a doctor utter it. I was well aware of the challenge this diagnosis would present.

Dr. Rubenstein continued talking, telling us that the chances of having triplets with autism was in the millions, and how in all his years in the field he'd seen it only twice. This distinction gave us no pleasure, however. In fact all the words that followed—how he believed that our move to Howard County was a wise choice, how the boys should have an Autism Diagnostic Observation Schedule test (ADOS) as well as genetic testing—existed in a wind tunnel. Given how far we had gone and how long we had sought a definitive answer, the diagnosis was somehow both anticlimactic and utterly devastating now that it had finally arrived.

We assumed that since their disorder had finally been named, we'd be given some kind of road map to follow. But by the time we were released from our cramped cell, we'd only received a pat on the back and a good luck. There were no prescriptions to fill, no agreed-upon treatment, no pamphlets, no road map.

We walked outside and stood a moment, blinking in the strong sunlight. The boys began crying inconsolably. What was wrong? There was too much noise and activity, too much information to process. I understood; we felt the same.

EVEN THOUGH I was the one who had pressed to verify the boys' diagnosis, in the days that followed I realized I was harboring a desperate secret hope that Dr. Stanley Greenspan, whom we were scheduled to see the next week, would come up with a different conclusion.

We felt exceedingly lucky to be able to see Dr. Greenspan at all. He was the originator of Floortime and the author of many books, and was considered an expert on the diagnosis and treatment of emotional and developmental disorders in infants and children. Even though we had great respect for Kennedy Krieger, I had built up high expectations for our Greenspan visit and the weight of a second professional opinion from him. Neither Greenspan nor Kennedy Krieger took our insurance, so these visits cost us thousands of dollars out of pocket.

Before our visit, we'd been asked to send Greenspan a video of the boys as toddlers. We'd sent a film Randy had made showing the boys playing and interacting and basically making a mess of our family room in the midst of normal toddler activities: Nicholas leafing through books, Zachary climbing the furniture, Hunter laughing as he played with his toys. I had also spoken extensively to the doctor's nurse beforehand, detailing the boys' medical history.

His office, attached to his residence on the outskirts of D.C., was cozy and inviting, with a waiting room filled with toys that the boys turned to with gusto. His nurse explained to us how the evaluation worked, then we were ushered in to speak to Dr. Greenspan himself, who told us that he would observe each boy singly.

Zachary was first, and Randy and I were asked to interact naturally with him—which was a little hard to do with this eminent expert studying us intently. The doctor particularly wanted to see how we were utilizing Floortime, the treatment program that was his brainchild.

We had heard previously that Dr. Greenspan might videotape us and we were prepared for this, but instead he simply sat in his chair and watched, occasionally providing suggestions, such as: "Why don't you try hiding that toy and asking Zachary to look for it?"

Between boys, Greenspan left the office, the first time returning with an egg salad sandwich, which he ate with gusto while we continued playing with the boys. At another point, he suddenly sat up erect in his chair and began doing arm lifts as if he were in a gymnasium.

Randy and I glanced at each other. Maybe he was a little eccentric, but he was considered one of the world's foremost authorities, so we didn't care whether he did somersaults.

There were long periods when the doctor didn't speak at all, but simply sat silently and watched. Again, I found it unnerving how purely observational this was. Part of me wanted someone to roll in an impressive piece of monitoring equipment, so some scan or image could be viewed and assessed. That this simple screening was the way our sons would be diagnosed didn't seem sophisticated or official enough.

But as the hours passed, we began to feel as if we were in the company of a great mind whose instincts we could trust, someone who was actually seeing us and making sense of our experience.

We already knew that unlike some professionals, who look at autism as a spectrum of deficits and excesses, Greenspan viewed it as a derailment of normal development. Floortime, his therapy intervention, was designed to determine exactly where the child had gone off track and then find a way to place him back on it again.

In the end Greenspan confirmed Kennedy Krieger's diagnosis, but he was much more upbeat about the boys' future improvement given our continued implementation of Floortime therapy.

He also was compassionate and uplifting, telling us that we were on the right track and that we were doing a great job with our sons. "You're good parents," he said. "Keep at it. Don't give up." These simple words were deeply nourishing; we needed all the hope we could find to sustain us.

So there it was; we had our definitive second opinion.

When we left Greenspan's office, a door long left half open finally slammed shut. The searching part of our journey was over.

11

THERAPY AND MORE THERAPY

The boys started summer school in the new school district and attended only a few days before coming down with scarlet fever, a disease I hadn't heard of since I read *Little Women* as a girl. Caused by a strep infection, each boy had the characteristic strawberry tongue, a florid pink with a pale center, and flushed cheeks. We withdrew them from summer school and decided to do a Floortime program and pay for an occupational therapist to help with gross and fine motor skills as well as sensory problems.

Meanwhile, getting services for the boys in our new county was not as easy or straightforward as we'd hoped. It turned out that the new school system was unwilling to accept the autism diagnosis from Greenspan and Krieger, which they considered a medical rather than an educational diagnosis. They wanted to evaluate the boys themselves to assess whether autism affected their learning.

From a financial point of view, they were simply being prudent.

Given their reputation for superior services, our new county had been flooded with special-needs children. An autism diagnosis equals costly services that a school system is required to supply until a child reaches twenty-one. Still, for us it meant more rounds of Individual Education Program meetings and endless evaluations.

We hired another educational consultant on our own at $150 an hour in order to navigate the complexities. Our hope was that the boys could attend upcoming kindergarten classes for half the day and spend the other half of the day in their home program, since we were unsure whether they could stay awake for so many hours. But the school thought it best for them to attend all day. Our consultant, a former teacher, thought we should waive the kindergarten year entirely and commence an intensive home program of applied behavior analysis—a widely used autism treatment that focuses on repetition and reward.

We decided to let the boys try a full day of kindergarten for several days, but just as we feared, it was a disaster. They were sleeping for three of the six hours they attended and weren't eating or drinking. We withdrew them and started a thirty-hour-a-week ABA program with a vendor generously supplied by the school system.

Before sequestering herself in the bedroom with a wailing Hunter the first day, the ABA aide said to me, "Don't come in, no matter how much he cries." What a thing to say to a mother!

The aide was trying to teach Hunter basic tasks: listening, paying attention, sitting in a chair. Yet from the sound of his wails, she was torturing him. I washed the dishes and did the laundry, trying to assess the tenor of his howls. One of the many things Randy and I have had to accept is that others can train our boys in ways that we are not always able.

By now our lives had become totally oriented toward the boys' therapies, as we tried to cram in as much treatment as possible. There was a wind at our backs, and we felt it. The boys were now five, fast approaching the end of the period when their brains were most "elastic" or changeable. Sorting out the various therapies, matching the correct version for each son, finding the right people to deliver them, and monitoring their success required constant vigilance and research. Randy and I had grown accustomed to having new people enter our house to work intimately with the boys, but it wasn't always easy or successful.

Ever since they were babies I've had a special frequency that picks up on any pain or unhappiness from the boys, and it was one of my hardest challenges to remain at the sink, my hands in suds, and not respond to Hunter's cries. Half of me was in that room, hugging and protecting him. But the other part was aware that in order to evolve into functional children, the boys had to undergo these treatments consistently and persistently.

Still, I had to make certain that the therapist was not pushing him too hard, that her doctrinaire attitude didn't cross over into harshness or abusiveness. Our boys don't present discipline problems and are not candidates for tough love.

On one occasion during therapy, the sound of Hunter's cries grew so distressed that I had to walk in and interrupt a therapy session. Meltdowns are not uncommon with autism, but it was my job to ascertain when they signify a problem, as this one did.

Hunter's face was scarlet, and he was visibly upset. I took one look at him and asked the therapist to leave our house. She was a young woman who hadn't been adequately trained to handle autism; whatever she had done had made Hunter completely distraught. In fact, he wouldn't enter his own bedroom for weeks afterward, and his anxiety about strangers increased.

Since the boys can't use language to tell us how they feel about situations, it has been up to Randy and me to be in tune with them and make certain they are happy, safe, and progressing. We have to be their voice until they can find their own.

THIS MONITORING of therapies and therapists may be challenging, but it is often the boys' intuitive sense about people that cues us in. Our sons are uncanny at judging characters and motives, and can often distinguish the good from the bad therapists straight away. Their body language is so eloquent that it's easy for me to pick up on their radar.

Hunter, who is not particularly trusting of people, simply resists going near someone he doesn't like. Nicholas is more dramatic and actually rolls his eyes and gives a *Here we go again* kind of look that says volumes. He also pivots and walks the other way if someone he dislikes is headed in his direction. On the other hand, when he *does* like someone, he's completely devoted, and he has often met favorite therapists at the door, grabbing them by the hand and leading them into his room.

The boys are occasionally so blunt about their preferences that it can result in awkward situations. Zachary simply asks for the therapist he wants by name, even if the person is not around.

"I want Diane," he announced stoutly one day, when his therapist Laura came to the door.

Oh, well. The purity of our boys, their directness and honesty, are virtues we value. If it causes bruised feelings, so be it. There are only so many ways the boys have to tell us how they feel, and we intend to honor them.

IN ORDER TO FACILITATE their in-home program, we set up the boys' bedrooms as mini therapy rooms, including oak tables and chairs. As part of the ABA vendor program each boy was assigned a main special-education teacher who headed the team and scheduled and trained technicians to implement the therapy. The entire team was overseen by a licensed psychologist who met with them regularly. Everybody had to be at the weekly meeting, including Randy, me, and the boys. Each team had at least two technicians who were college students looking to launch a career helping children with special needs.

Our house soon resembled a bustling dorm, a revolving door of college students with backpacks and cell phones, coming and going seven days a week. Occasionally, there seemed to be more going than coming, as it dawned on some of these students that working with children with autism was *not* as easy as it might appear.

ABA is a demanding treatment that requires repetition and consistency for hours on end. We could quickly tell which students were going to last by the way they approached our sons and spoke to them. If they sauntered in, acting as if this were a babysitting job, we knew they wouldn't last.

And there were other challenges, outside our home. Just when we thought we might be able to relax for a moment, there would be a reminder that our advocacy could never end.

One reminder came when a school psychologist, who was simply sitting in on an IEP meeting and had never met the boys before, informed us that they should be labeled as multiply disabled instead of autisic. I watched him studying the boys' records, looking up at us from under his glasses. This change would have been a major step back for us, an unraveling of all the work we had done so far to have them correctly diagnosed. I could almost see the years of visits, phone calls, and long waits gurgling down the drain.

Hearing this stranger coolly discuss the dismantling of all our work, seeing how he wasn't even able to differentiate one boy from another, I appreciated for the first time what it meant to see red. I didn't care what kind of Ph.D. this guy had. We had been saddled with the enormous misdiagnosis of MR for Hunter and Nicholas for two long years, and had only recently had the label removed after months of arduous work.

When I finally spoke, I felt as if I were ten feet tall and breathing fire. "Our boys have autism, and they're quite capable of learning. There's no way I'm going to let them be labeled anything else."

Both the teacher and the autism specialist for Howard County, who knew our boys best, concurred that the boys' disability should be autism.

Still, I could feel Randy turning to look at me, wondering whatever had happened to the compliant peacemaker he'd married.

Well, she was long gone by now.

• • •

IT WAS around this time that we started looking for a DAN! (Defeat Autism Now!) doctor. We'd read that they stressed biomedical approaches to autism and were known to work more closely with parents than conventional physicians did.

We investigated locally, and to my amazement one of the DAN! doctors listed on a website was my very own childhood pediatrician, and not only mine but also my brother's and my sister's.

Thus ended our search. This was a man with whom my whole family had a history of trust. We called his office on a holiday weekend, and he returned our call within hours and told us to come right over to his office.

"He calls us right back. He wants to see us on a holiday weekend. *And* he takes medical insurance." Randy couldn't believe it.

Seeing him again after so many years was heartwarming. This was the man who had escorted us through the stumbles and illnesses of childhood. He looked the same to me, kindly if a bit silvered. He was so attentive to the boys and took the whole afternoon examining them and talking with us. He told us that he wanted us to collect urine, hair, and stool samples for lab testing.

He also took the time to explain to us in detail what he would be looking for in the test results. He spoke in such scientific detail that I found myself digging back in my memory to those chemistry and anatomy classes I had taken in school.

When we left the office, Randy looked at his watch in amazement. "We've been there all afternoon," he said.

It wasn't easy obtaining urine, hair, and stool samples for three overactive boys, but in the following days, we managed it and sent them to the lab.

Upon receiving the test results, the doctor told us that the boys had various vitamin deficiencies and chemical toxicities and should start building their immune systems with a variety of supplements. Vitamin C, TMG, SuperNuThera, probiotics, and cod liver oil were some of the first recommendations, which we found at holistic health stores.

Within days of administering some of these supplements—SuperNuThera, for example—we began seeing results. Hunter and Zachary were noticeably more verbal, and Nicholas began making more eye contact and engaging with us.

The fact that this kind of intervention could make such a difference opened up a new world for us.

THAT HALLOWEEN, we dressed the boys as a trio of superheroes—Batman, Spider-Man, and Superman—and took them trick-or-treating around the neighborhood.

Zachary had really gotten the knack of Halloween by that time: He understood that after he knocked on a door he was supposed to say "Trick or treat!" and hold out his bag with a smile. But Hunter and Nicholas still didn't quite comprehend it and were in sensory overload from having attended a Halloween party earlier in the day. Still, they seemed to enjoy the novelty of being dressed up in strange clothes and taking a walk as a family. But whenever a neighbor opened the door, they stood blankly in their little outfits and let Zachary do the honors.

Around that time, Nicholas had been experiencing trouble

sleeping through the night and had developed a ferocious, man-sized snore that reverberated throughout the house. It turned out that his tonsils were the culprit, and we scheduled to have them removed, along with his adenoid, during outpatient surgery.

My mother came over and watched Zachary and Hunter for the morning while Randy and I took Nicholas to the local hospital. While he was in pre-op he began making sounds as we dressed him in his hospital gown. They sounded like "Buuhhh." I knew this meant he wanted something to drink before surgery, which wasn't allowed. The more we told him he couldn't have anything, the louder his sounds became.

A young female doctor with auburn hair and a kind face peeked around the curtain curiously. "Does your son have autism?" she asked.

I was a little taken aback by the question, but her sweet manner won me over. "Yes, how could you tell?"

The doctor said, "He's making the exact same sounds as my son does—it's so surreal." She smiled down at Nicholas as lovingly as if he were her son. I found it amazing that she could pick up that Nicholas had autism simply by the sounds he was making.

We all stood there for a moment, united in a circle of affection. It was one of our more frequently occurring peeks at the bond that exists between parents with special-needs children. Autism changes you: the way you look at other children, the way you look at each other as parents, the way you are transformed on a dime into educational advocates. It was moments like this that made Randy and me more certain than ever that the Autism Expo we had been planning for months was a crucial event.

•   •   •

AFTER SPENDING a quiet Thanksgiving at home that year—no company, no confusion—we began to wonder whether the boys were improving sufficiently from the rigid ABA program and whether an applied verbal behavior program might be a better fit, especially for Nicholas and Hunter.

Because the ABA program started at such a basic level, our sons were able to do many of the common tasks, such as looking, listening, and imitating, but they still lacked the expressive and conversational language of their peers.

Our sons' core deficit was speech, and applied verbal behavior was designed to target that. AVB also worked within the child's natural environment and was based on what motivates him to communicate.

Our sons' lack of language was our largest concern, and we worried that time was running out for them to acquire this fundamental skill. We wanted our boys to be able to complain about their stomachaches, to tell us what they were thinking and dreaming, why they were happy or sad. Language was key to their future independent lives.

We made the determination about applied verbal behavior ourselves, from our independent research and talking to other parents. But making the switch wasn't going to be easy; it meant dealing with the school system and changing providers, which could be a touchy maneuver.

Our private educational consultant thought perhaps the boys should be in a specialized school for autistic children where whatever program we chose would be intensive and consistent instead of linked with a rotating turnover of college students.

She advised us to speak to the special-education attorney we hired earlier in the year and gain his input. The attorney agreed to let the school system know we wanted to change providers or to find an appropriate school setting for them.

Just as we feared, both the school and our current vendor were unhappy to hear that we wanted to change the boys' placement. When we met to discuss these changes, the gathering was fraught with such tension and defensiveness that I could feel them, like electricity, in the air.

At an earlier time, I would have been distraught about upsetting any of them. But hurt feelings and bruised egos were nothing next to our boys' futures. It wasn't that I didn't care about how other people felt, but over the years I had forged a resolve and focus when it came to our sons. They couldn't stand up for themselves or chart their own futures. They counted on Randy and me to navigate this world for them. Without us, they would be lost.

So I sat in the meeting and listened to the objections and observed the flushed faces, but Randy and I were now a united front and we stood our ground.

That winter, while still in limbo, we acted ourselves, and set up a home AVB program with a local service provider that sent an in-home program consultant named Renee. Unfortunately, once we withdrew the boys from the ABA program, we had to assume the financial burden for the new therapy. But the benefits of this program far outweighed the costs. Our instincts had been right; under Renee's inspired approach, our sons were "manding" up a storm within a few weeks. A "mand" is a request, the function of which is to obtain what's desired. So if a child says "candy cane," and it is functioning as a mand, that means the child is requesting a candy cane.

To see the boys desire something—a cracker, a video, a toy— and have their own way of asking for and receiving it—was a deep satisfaction for us, and a proud breakthrough for them.

• • •

12

VACCINES VERSUS DNA

One topic that had been burning in our minds all along—and that no doctor had previously broached—was the cause of our son's autism. We felt as compelled to explore what had caused the boys' condition as we were to treat it. Yet this was another subject cloaked in apprehension and silence.

We had discovered that the debate about autism's cause was highly emotional and deeply divided the autism community. There were two main divisions and much shading in between—those who believed that the growing number of autism cases had been triggered by vaccines and the preservative contained in them, the mercury-based thimerosal, and others who believed in a primarily genetic basis.

It seemed sad to us that such division and anger existed between parties who shared an important concern—the welfare of children with autism.

When we returned to Kennedy Krieger that winter, we met with a leading neurologist in the field, Dr. Andrew Zimmerman, who told us that he thought that our boys' autism was probably the result of genetic factors combined with a social or toxic trigger.

The first evidence of a genetic basis for autism came from a 1977 twin study that showed that if one twin had the disorder, the other was far more likely to have it if he was identical than if he was fraternal. Fraternal twins share only about half of their DNA, while identical ones, like Hunter and Nicholas, share all. But through all the intervening years, it had still proven difficult for researchers to discover the exact genes that were involved.

Some researchers suspect that a faulty gene or genes might make a person vulnerable to develop autism in the presence of other triggering factors.

Many triggers had been suggested, from viruses and pesticides, to pet shampoos, chemicals in cosmetics and foods, older parents, and stress. But probably the most widely suspected triggers were vaccines—either the preservatives in them or their sheer number. We had read and worried over every possibility.

Zimmerman also mentioned that there was research looking into the possibility that in vitro fertilization, and the regimen of vaccines and hormones associated with it, could have created a toxic early environment for our boys before they even entered the world.

We were glad to have these conversations, but our curiosity was hardly satisfied. The cause of our sons' disorder continued to haunt us, though in our hearts we didn't believe that genetics played a role. We had no autism in our families, and each boy had been affected differently. Furthermore, our boys had been perfectly normal for the first eighteen months of life. Had they been born with these deficits, it would have been different. But we had witnessed the great shift, as if some force had entered the room and yanked them back in time.

When we looked at photos of the boys at six months, then two years, we saw the visible regression. Like any other parents in such a situation, we couldn't help agonizing over what had happened to them and why.

Vaccinations were the one thing that stood out in our minds. The more we thought about it over the years, the more we were haunted by the fact that our premature infants were injected with hepatitis B vaccines when they were only days old.

Added to this, our boys had many more vaccinations than the typical child. At our pediatrician's urging, they received the flu vaccine for the first two years of their lives as well as a Synagis vaccine from October through March for the first two years in order to prevent respiratory syncytial virus, commonly referred to as RSV. One of our DAN! doctors believed that this sheer number of vaccinations could have impaired the immune system of our boys, ultimately triggering their autism. In other words, it was too many, too soon, for their little bodies to eliminate.

If I knew then what I know now is always a poignant rumination for a parent of autistic children, since the costs of wrong moves and lost time are especially potent for us.

Some nights when I lay in bed, I imagined stopping time and going back to those early days when I was so blindly trusting of our doctors. In these scenes I walk into the examining room and say something I never uttered in real life: "No, enough."

I take the needles from her hand and say, "Our boys are four-pound preemies, they need time to catch up." I say: "I want you to space out the essential vaccines, but I don't want you to give them anything extra." I am eloquent and strong in these imaginary scenes.

Vaccines are an extremely difficult issue for us. It breaks our hearts to think that we might have done anything whatsoever that could have negatively impacted our boys. For a doting, protective mother like me, who so carefully watched over her sons and responded to their every whimper and cry, the notion that an intervention we consented to may have harmed the boys is particularly wrenching. Still, we wanted to know. As Randy has often said: "There's something affecting these children at that age, and it's unfortunate that families are left to their own devices to find out what it is."

We had also been alerted to the possibility of an underlying mitochondrial disorder in the boys, a neuromuscular disease caused by damage to the mitochondria (energy-producing structures that serve as the cells' power plants) that is set off by some kind of environmental influence.

We had grown more concerned about this possibility following the landmark legal case of a Georgia girl, Hannah Poling. In 2008, the federal government agreed to compensate the nine-year-old, conceding that the five vaccinations she received had "significantly aggravated an underlying mitochondrial disorder," which eventually manifested as a brain disease with autistic features.

Like our boys, Poling had been developing normally at nineteen months when she received five vaccinations against nine infectious diseases. Within two days, she'd developed a fever and was unable to walk. Poling's family contended that the mercury-based preservatives in the vaccines she received may have damaged her mitochondria. When these specialized compartments don't work properly, they can cause organ damage and failure. Symptoms in infants include seizures and delayed motor and mental development, along with hearing and eye movement problems.

Poling's case gave credence to the theory that vaccinations can trigger or unmask an underlying mitochondrial disorder by causing the body to mount an immune response, in turn causing autism.

The Poling case became important because it alerted us to other cases of mitochondrial disorder that resembled our boys' trajectory: long periods of normal development followed by regression. Just as disturbing was a second, more recent case. This involved a six-year-old Colorado girl who received a flu vaccine and a week later grew weak, developed difficulty walking, and eventually died after several months. Like Hannah Poling, this girl had also suffered from mitochondrial disorders.

These cases gave us new information about this syndrome just at the time when our own boys were beginning to exhibit frightening new symptoms—leading us to fear that something else was happening medically with them. Nicholas had begun developing gastrointestinal problems as well as unexplained vomiting during the day. Zachary was showing signs of regressions and nightmares as well as momentary seizures. But Hunter's symptoms were the most terrifying.

One evening, Hunter had fallen asleep a little early after a busy day at school. He suddenly sat up in a somewhat comatose fashion and began screaming a blood-curdling cry that was different from his normal tired cry and more a wail of extreme pain. His cries grew in intensity as his body began to convulse. He went into a complete state of duress, arching his back and flopping around uncontrollably. His blanket was in his mouth, and bands of tears streamed down his cheeks as his eyes rolled white.

Terrified, Randy and I both desperately maneuvered around him to stop his flailing body. Hunter grabbed Randy's arms and hands as if to plead for some sort of intercession. It was as if his body were being continually jolted by lightning. He stiffened, then calmed, only to do this over and over. Finally, he lay still in our arms for an hour until he fell asleep again. He was incapable of telling us in words the way he felt yet his actions made it obvious that he had been in great pain and duress.

There is nothing more frightening than watching one's child helplessly suffer and not know how to help or stop it. After these incidents, Randy and I became increasingly convinced that the boys might be suffering from some other medical condition, such as mitochondrial disorder, in addition to, or in conjunction with, their autism—a terrifying new possibility.

But like so much involving autism, getting tested for mitochondrial disorders was exceedingly difficult. There were only three experts in the country, and they did not take walk-ins but only critical referrals from leading neurologists. We had been told by the boys' neurologist that the boys had no "markers" for mitochondrial disorder, but a true diagnosis involved a costly and invasive muscle biopsy, so we found ourselves back at square one.

We had also been wondering about fragile X—a genetic condition that can cause mental impairment. Approximately one-third of all children diagnosed with fragile X syndrome also have some degree of autism. Because this could be tested through a simple blood sample, we decided to proceed.

Though they wouldn't change the fact that the boys had autism, the results might alter the treatment; they also might give us an idea regarding the central mystery of their lives, what had caused their autism in the first place.

WHILE GOVERNMENT OFFICIALS insisted the Hannah Poling case was an "anomaly," Randy showed me news reports that the government had been settling vaccine injury cases since the early nineties, though maintaining to the public that there was no cause for worry. Furthermore, the landmark CDC study that had found no link between mercury in vaccines and autism—the one that was so widely cited and embedded in the public's consciousness—had been deemed flawed in methodology and data.

I felt a sheen of sweat cover me as I sat and read these reports, and a memory floated back to me from a decade before. It was a scene with my father when he was gravely ill with multiple myeloma. We had just left the office of a doctor who had told him he had six months to live. As I followed my father out the office door, I remember being struck by how strong he was; I thought of all the lessons he'd passed on to me over the years.

"There's no 'I can't,'" he used to tell me. "Only 'I'll try.'"

He didn't just say this, he lived it, and he continued to do so for the rest of his life, undergoing a number of cancer surgeries as well as dialysis three times a week. In fact, he survived five more years after that doctor's grim prognosis, stunning everyone with his grit and determination.

So much of the conventional wisdom I'd heard throughout my lifetime had been wrong, and now, according to this document, the very study that had so often been used to silence our concerns was flawed.

How often had we been told, "There's no link between vaccines and autism. The government says so," whenever we'd voiced concerns about vaccinations?

How many times had we gone back home feeling foolish and then sat together watching the sons whom we loved beyond all measure struggle with the deficits and limitations that had been visited upon them?

My intuition, our gut instincts and inner knowledge—I would never ignore them again.

The whole tenor of the autism debate, in fact, had changed since our boys first regressed. Now people were talking not so much about whether vaccinations were the trigger but what role vaccinations might play.

• • •

13

BECOMING AUTISM ADVOCATES

Before he left for work one day in February 2007, Randy showed me a newspaper headline, stating that the CDC had released startling new figures increasing the number of children being diagnosed with autism from 1 in 166 to a new figure—1 in 150.

I felt a jolt as I read it. Despite our busy life, we were becoming increasingly aware that there were thousands of families out there going through exactly what we were, albeit on a smaller scale.

The phone rang later that morning as I was making a second pot of coffee. It was Randy, now at work: "How would you like to be on TV this afternoon?"

I laughed. "Oh sure, as what—the world's most exhausted mother?"

"I'm serious."

I still didn't believe him, but it turned out he was telling the truth. *NBC Nightly News with Brian Williams* wanted to interview us about the new CDC statistics as well as film the boys.

How did they even know about us? It turned out that while a public relations contact of ours named Lisa Miles was publicizing our upcoming Expo, the media were becoming increasingly curious about our family and the boys in particular.

I looked up into the mirror and caught a glimpse of not only myself but the landscape of our living room—the boys sitting in the midst of toys, clothes, videos, and books.

"What time?" I asked Randy.

"If we agree, they'll be there in two hours. I think we should do it."

I took a swallow and said, "Okay," then hung up and began tearing through the house, tidying up, dressing the boys, and trying to get myself together. All the while, I was asking myself, *Why in the world does anyone want to interview us?*

We had never considered ourselves exceptional but simply devoted parents, slogging through a terrain that wasn't easy, but that was just our lives.

In fact, the CDC numbers seemed to have caused some tipping point in the public consciousness; now so many people wanted to hear about us. After the interview aired the next day, our local affiliates picked up the story from the evening news. Two local television stations were interested in interviewing us on the same day. The Baltimore *Sun* and *Examiner* and *The Washington Post* also were interested. Soon we found ourselves accustomed to opening the door to reporters and camera equipment. After feeling isolated for so long, suddenly a light was shining on us.

• • •

OUR OTHER VENTURE into the outer world was the long-planned Autism Expo. Randy called it a labor of love, and he wasn't kidding. Once it was over, neither of us quite knew how we'd found the time to organize this event in the middle of our busy lives. But between naps and snatched moments, we had done it. And there we were at Howard Community College on April 14, 2007, and the auditorium was packed.

Our main impetus all along had been to help families in the overwhelming early months following diagnosis when they were confronted with the need to rapidly find therapies and treatments for their child's unique deficits. Not only did we remember how it felt to be under the gun the moment our kids were diagnosed but we were still struggling with these same issues.

Our goal had been to bring together experts, teachers, parents, doctors, and therapists all in one place, and that's what we'd done. Dr. Vincent Carbone, a renowned expert in the field, was on hand to give the keynote speech. Kennedy Krieger Institute, Pathfinders for Autism, and the National Institutes of Health were participating as vendors, among many others.

We had DAN! doctors, educational attorneys, speech and occupational therapists, and doctors from the genetics lab at Duke University. We had Dr. Janelle Love with her hyperbaric chamber, a pressurized tube that forces large quantities of oxygen into the body and, some believe, improves autism symptoms, and Dr. Pamela J. Compart, who researches nutrient deficiencies and digestive problems in autistic children.

Everywhere I turned, I saw parents huddled together, talking, exchanging phone numbers and e-mail addresses; nowhere in that auditorium did I find a single face of despair.

At one point I looked over and saw Randy, his face alight, in such deep conversation with a young man that I couldn't help wondering whom he was talking to. When I found out, I understood. The young man was Stephen Shore, author of *Beyond the Wall* and *Autism for Dummies*. Articulate and successful, Shore was a young man with autism who had achieved great things, including, recently, his Ed.D. In him, Randy found a role model for our sons and the vast possibilities for their futures.

We hadn't realized that this Expo would be just as meaningful for us, the organizers, as for the parents who packed the rooms, hungry for information and advice. If we had closed our eyes and imagined what we had most yearned for during those tough early years, this would have been it—an educational exchange of so much information, everyone respectful and interested in varying views and approaches. Our connections from the Expo gave us strength and hope to set up a web of support that we draw from still.

NOT MANY SIX-YEAR-OLD BOYS appear on the front page of the Sunday early edition of *The Washington Post* for their birthdays, but that year Zachary did. He smiled when we pointed out his sweet face, there with the news and weather and stock market prices. He didn't know what it meant, but we did. Autism had finally pierced the public's awareness. It was a worldwide concern now, not just ours.

After the story ran, we received piles of correspondence, and read the same phrases over and over: "We couldn't figure out what was wrong with our son. . . . It took us years to get diagnosed. . . . Thanks for telling your story."

Randy and I sat under the light in the kitchen and read these letters late into the night, passing them back and forth. The kids were asleep above us, the dryer was humming in the laundry room, the kitchen still smelled like that night's pepperoni pizza. It was a regular weeknight, with one difference: It had finally registered in us that we were not alone.

•   •   •

14

A BREAKTHROUGH AND A TRIUMPH

Our new county had a reputation for being a kind of Grace-
land for children with autism, a haven for families who'd
been as starved for services as we had been. People from all over
the country were streaming into the area because the schools were
top-notch for neurotypical children and the bar was held so high
for those with special needs. We sensed that we might have finally
found the right place, but we were still somewhat wary given our
previous experiences.

We had already heard rare reviews about a pilot program the
county had implemented called Multiple Intensive Needs Classroom—Errorless Learning (MINC-EL). It sounded like a perfect
fit for Hunter and Nicholas, and Randy arranged for them to be
assessed.

One summer morning we took both boys to the local public
school and met Melanie, the autism specialist, and Shannon, the
MINC-EL teacher.

Our hearts opened as we watched both Shannon and Melanie take turns playing with the boys and as they asked us astute and perceptive questions about their capabilities. We were so accustomed to having the real nature of the boys' condition ignored, misdiagnosed, unrecognized, or belittled. But these women didn't find the boys baffling or mysterious. They understood what they were seeing. What a difference from our old school system.

We had never encountered a teacher like Shannon before—one who took such an interest in our boys, who seemed to be so competent as well as well genuinely caring and kind. The boys, with their tender antennae, picked up on this too. By the end of the meeting it was decided that Nicholas and Hunter were in fact perfect for the pilot program. We didn't realize at the time that Shannon would also become the boys' teacher, thus raising the bar for all others in the future.

The only difficulty was that when the IEP team met in August and finalized this placement, it was determined that Zachary should be placed in the regular kindergarten program at the local elementary school. We were thrilled with this placement, but it meant that our boys would now be split up in separate schools that were miles apart and in opposite directions. This threw our daily schedule, already onerous, into chaos. I still felt uncomfortable placing the boys on the bus, and even if I drove like a maniac, there was no way that I could get them all to school on time.

Randy went to his boss and requested that his work hours be changed so that he could help me with transportation; his boss went one step further, also allowing Randy to work from home when he needed to.

During the next months in the new school system, we were able to make headway in other areas where we'd been stymied. Zachary's disability was finally changed from developmental delay to autism. Nicholas and Hunter flourished in their new environment using applied verbal behavior methods; Nicholas also thrived with the picture exchange system known as PECS.

For the first time, we felt that we were able to entrust our boys with professionals who were sympathetic and qualified. After so many years of worrying about the boys being ignored, misunderstood, or bullied, I drove away from them in the morning without that awful queasy anxiety. For this alone, the move to Howard County had been worthwhile.

In the meantime, publicity continued to build around us, and we became accustomed to handling media requests, something that would have been unthinkable a year before. Had anyone told me that our family would ever be featured on *Good Morning America*, I would not have believed it. But that's exactly what happened one hot sultry day in August when a camera crew came out and spent a good part of a day with us. Randy and I had agreed that any chance to raise autism awareness was a plus for our sons; the more the public was aware of autism, the more people would be willing to give our kids a chance. Later that year, we also filmed a public service announcement for Kennedy Krieger on the first anniversary of the IAN project, a national database that collects data to share with researchers for future studies.

IN SEPTEMBER, Nicholas began experiencing severe stomach pains and vomiting. The pediatrician suggested that it might simply be gas or constipation. But I had serious doubts; the pain appeared to be sharp and severe enough that he grabbed at his stomach and wept. This was another reminder, if I needed one, why language was so crucial for our boys to master; without it, we only had these mute and heartbreaking pantomimes of pain. Nicholas could not tell any doctor exactly where he hurt or how much. But as his mother, I was acutely aware of his discomfort and felt so helpless. Soft drinks occasionally seemed to ease his pain, which ebbed and flowed, based on what, we could not imagine.

And then, as if in answer to some silent prayer, a patch of blue suddenly broke through, and we had a breakthrough and triumph. One February morning I was in the kitchen getting Hunter a glass of juice from the refrigerator when I felt Nicholas tugging at the back of my shirt, the kind of gesture he often used to communicate. Today, he was especially insistent and kept pulling on my shirt.

"Just a minute, honey."

He kept pulling. Then out of the blue I heard a faint voice say, "Mama."

I turned around and looked at him. I thought I was hearing things. "Did you *say* something?"

Nicholas looked at me, and said it again, easy as pie: "Mama, mama."

I scooped him up into my arms and burst into tears, kissing and hugging him. It had been almost five years since we'd heard that sweet voice. For all that time, we had been bound together by our own private sign language. Many professionals had tried to convince us that he had passed the age when we could expect his speech to return, but we hadn't given up on him.

What had finally made him find his words again? Was it removing dairy products from his diet? Was it the countless hours of intensive therapies? Was it our refusal to follow the school's advice and place him on a voice box? Was it our belief? Or was it just Nicholas's time?

I was heartsick that Randy was at the grocery, unable to share this long-awaited moment. I called him on the cell phone. As soon as he picked up, I began crying into the receiver. "You're not going to believe this!"

He remained silent, unsure whether the news was going to be good or bad.

"Listen to this." I held up the phone, and Nicholas murmured, "Mama."

There was still silence on the other end. We hadn't heard him speak for so long that Randy didn't recognize the sound.

"Did you hear him?"

"Hear *who?*"

"It's Nick, he's speaking!" I cried. "Come home, drop the groceries. He's speaking!"

"You're kidding! Can you get him to do it again!"

I was afraid Nicholas might have dried up, but I held him close and whispered. "Daddy wants to hear it again. Talk again for Daddy."

And as if he understood just how important this was for us, he spoke with a long clear: "Mammmmma."

Now Randy and I were beyond words ourselves, sniffling over the receiver as Nicholas, on a roll now, kept repeating his sole word. This was the moment we'd been striving for—if we could get him to say one word, we knew that he'd be able to say another.

"Yes!" Randy cried. I heard a kind of euphoria in my husband's voice that I hadn't heard since we'd first become pregnant and viewed our boys on the sonogram. For the first time in years, we and Nicholas were on speaking terms again.

AND THERE WERE other bright spots in the following months, moments to savor. In fact, when you have a child with autism, you learn to relish the smallest milestone, things that other people take for granted: your child picking a cup off the floor and placing it on the table, running into your arms when you pick him up from school. Seeing Zachary write his name for the first time with his big pencil, concentrating as hard as if he were scrawling a mathematical formula; Hunter turning to us out of the blue on his birthday and blurting out, "I love you," a phrase we had waited years to hear. Witnessing Nicholas erupt from the school astride a bike for the first time, his proud teachers arrayed behind him as he pedaled independently.

But hearing Nicholas's voice again after four long years of silence was perhaps the greatest moment of all. The way it felt to hear him say *Mama* that day was something that I, the verbal one, have no way to adequately articulate.

BY FEBRUARY, Nicholas had had a CAT scan on his stomach because of his continuing pain. A blockage was found on the right side of his intestine—a potentially dangerous situation. Once the pediatric gastroenterologist we visited learned that Nicholas had autism and couldn't verbally describe his pain to her, her demeanor turned cool and dismissive. She put him on a medication, Miralax, that gave him some relief, but he was still experiencing daily pain. When we called to tell her this, she seemed perplexed and disinterested. In case we had been lulled into thinking that we were in for smooth sailing now that we'd moved, this experience reminded us that our support for the boys would have to continue until they could speak for themselves.

In the meantime, our worry extended to Hunter, who, along with his terrifying seizure, had been failing to gain weight all year, despite the fact that he ate all the time and had the most balanced meals of all the boys. He also seemed to be falling ill more frequently—with diarrhea, fever, and vomiting. When we took him to his regular pediatrician, he thought that it was a virus, but fourteen days of nonstop diarrhea seemed to be more than that to us.

He was admitted at Kennedy Krieger for an overnight EEG and genetic testing. Fragile X wasn't detected, only a vitamin D deficiency. We decided to consult a DAN! doctor, Dr. Pamela Compart, for further advice. DAN! doctors are known take a more holistic, biomedical approach, looking at diet, nutrition, and supplements.

Two years before, we'd consulted another DAN! doctor. He had advised us to take the boys off dairy, as well as eliminate certain foods from their diets and add supplements, and we'd seen some progress.

Our new doctor was also a developmental pediatrician, and she was responsive and thorough. She started a more aggressive DAN! protocol for Hunter after he seemed to be in a lot of pain from the vitamin D deficiency. She looked over all of Hunter's test results and prescribed a list of supplements, and he quickly responded.

THAT APRIL, we filed our taxes online as we normally do, and received notification that our return was rejected because someone had already filed, using one of our Social Security numbers. When Randy called the IRS early that morning, he was told that it was *my* Social Security number that had been used. We were instructed to bring all documentation verifying my identity with us to the nearest IRS office and file an identity theft report.

When we met with the IRS agent in Annapolis, he told us that my ID had been stolen by someone who claimed to be a single female college student with a New York City apartment. The agent gave us a copy of the fraudulent return and told us that we needed to file a police report, contact all three credit reporting agencies to put a fraud alert on my credit report, and contact all my financial institutions. The officer also told us that the theft was part of an elaborate ruse, an "inside job."

"Make sure you shred your trash from now on," he said.

It was all unsettling, a kind of violation—the sense that some stranger had been rooting through my life, might even be committing crimes in my name. As the days passed, I kept wondering what else might turn up—whether I'd receive a bill for a new Mercedes convertible or a full-length fur coat. But nothing else happened, except for the massive inconvenience and a nonexistent tax refund.

Still during those weeks I couldn't help imagining what it would be like to have an alternate glittering life in Manhattan—eating out and going to museums, having no one to worry about but myself. It was an interesting diversion during all the hassle.

And then as quickly as it had started, it was over. I walked out to get the mail one afternoon, and there was my credit report. I ripped it open, and all was clear. Whoever this person was, she had moved on and disappeared.

I walked back into the house, where Randy was sitting in the middle of the living room floor with all three boys, and I stopped a moment, as if seeing my life from this stranger's viewpoint, perceiving it all for the first time.

The living room was a mess of computer books, a mini trampoline, and a laptop computer. Randy was doing what he always does somehow, engaging all three boys at the same time—one arm around Hunter, the other touching Nicholas's arm, one leg bolstering Zachary.

Nicholas spoke for one week after that exciting afternoon, and then he stopped; he hasn't said anything since. But now he looks over his shoulder at me standing in the doorway and gives me a gleaming look of such love that my throat tightens.

The truth is that I couldn't imagine any other life. These four souls were my family, and I wouldn't trade them for any glittering existence in Manhattan. This is our world, and these boys our blessings. We'll continue to fight for them—for their speech and health and advancement—for the rest of our days. Nicholas's smile, for this second of this Tuesday, is more than enough.

PART TWO

• • •

NOT A ROAD MAP
BUT A PATH

Much has improved in the world of autism during the six years since our boys began their regression. There is now increased research and funding as well as awareness of the autism spectrum disorders, though this has hardly kept pace with the growing incidence—1 in 150 children now being affected.

One of the most heartening advancements to us personally has been the emergence of a collective voice of parents who have banded together to help each other and demand change. Through blogs and the contacts we made at our Autism Expo, Randy and I now have people we can confide in and turn to for advice. We are no longer a closed unit, and this is an immense comfort to us.

But the fact remains there is still no road map, no single treatment or intervention that can be recommended for every child suffering from autism. An individualized approach, based on a child's unique needs, is still the reality—time-consuming and frustrating as it may be.

Still, with three sons on the spectrum, we've tried or researched many of the possible interventions. We may not have a well-lit paved road as a result, but we do have a well-trod path. In this section, we give our take on some of the hard truths we've learned on our journey, as well as treatment options and resources.

• • •

15

TWENTY THINGS EVERY PARENT SHOULD KNOW

As a parent of autistic children, you soon realize that there are some truths that only other parents who've been in your exact situation can tell you. Here are a few of the essential truths we've gleaned along the way.

1. EVERY CHILD WITH AUTISM IS UNIQUE

There's a saying that if you have met one child with autism, you have met one child with autism.

That is because the spectrum of autism disorders is so wide and diverse. It ranges from those with significant impairments—who may be silent and locked into hand-flapping and rocking—to higher-functioning children with Asperger's syndrome, who have no general delay in language or cognitive development but may have odd or limited social skills. In our family alone, our sons exhibit three different manifestations—our silent son, Nicholas; our middle-range son, Hunter; and Zachary, who has been diagnosed with Asperger's and is the highest-functioning.

Because there are so many types of autism, each case is unique, and every child will respond differently to treatments and therapies.

2. EARLY INTERVENTION IS CRUCIAL

We cannot stress enough the importance of early diagnosis and intervention. The sooner your child is diagnosed, the sooner he or she can benefit from therapy and services, which are particularly crucial during the early years of life.

There is no medical test for autism. It is diagnosed by observing a child's behavior, communication skills, and interactions with others. The challenge is that the symptoms of autism are so varied and usually occur in the first two years of life, when a child's personality is just beginning to emerge.

As a parent, you are the one most likely to pick up on the following early warning signs of autism:

- Delay or loss of speech and social skills
- Sustained repetitive behaviors
- Avoidance of eye contact
- Obsession with routines
- Fascination with parts of objects
- Difficulty developing friendships
- Lack of response to sound or hearing name; appearing deaf

- Echoing of words or phrases
- Does not want cuddling
- Prefers being alone
- Lack of pretend play
- Inappropriate play with toys, such as spinning wheels of a toy truck over and over
- Poor social, physical, and verbal skills
- Tiptoe walking
- Need for sameness
- Need to carry objects everywhere with them
- Sleep problems that cannot be resolved with traditional remedies
- Flapping arms continuously for no apparent reason
- Spinning in circles without becoming dizzy
- Need to have everything in place
- No single words by sixteen months
- No two-word sentences by age two
- Easily upset without cause
- Overreaction or underreaction to sensory stimuli
- Lack of fear of danger
- Difficulty in carrying on a conversation

3. TRUST YOUR OWN INSTINCTS

No one knows a child like you, the parent. You are the leading expert. Trust your own gut when it comes to your child. Randy and I spent years strongly suspecting that our boys had autism before we could find a professional to concur with us.

We found it exhausting and exasperating shuttling the boys from specialist to specialist. But we knew that time was not on our side and that we were our boys' gatekeeper to the world of treatment options.

Speak up and insist on being heard. If a particular doctor or professional won't listen to your concerns, try another; get a second or third opinion.

4. BECOME ACCUSTOMED TO TEAMWORK

Raising a child with autism requires a group approach. It will not be possible for you to fulfill all the needs of your child on your own. No one person will have all the answers you're looking for.

When your child receives an autism diagnosis, you'll find yourself consulting a myriad of experts—from medical professionals to special-education attorneys—to make certain your child is receiving all the help he or she deserves.

A few of the therapists we have employed for our boys include physical, occupational, behavioral, speech-language, and play. Each of these professionals will want to know your child's developmental history, so make sure to keep one that is up to date on hand.

Having both medical and educational data handy will be key in monitoring your child's progress. It's a good idea to keep the data in a three-ring binder, separated by date and treatment. If you are technically savvy you can also store it electronically in case you need to communicate via e-mail.

5. KNOW YOUR CHILD'S RIGHTS

Special-education law can be complex, but as the gatekeeper to your child's future, you need to understand it. School systems and educators may not offer the information to you freely.

What the IDEA Is

The Individuals with Disabilities Education Act (IDEA) is a law mandating that the state provide all eligible children with a free and appropriate public education (FAPE) that meets their unique individual needs in the least restrictive environment (LRE).

If a child meets the state eligibility requirements that define disability (and autism is considered a disability), the IDEA says that a child is legally entitled to receive early intervention services or special-education services.

If you are a parent, a role has been established in the IDEA for you as the planner and monitor of your child's Individual Education Program.

What an IFSP Is

If a child has been diagnosed with autism and is less than three years old, the first educational placement is usually through an early intervention program.

Early intervention services are geared toward minimizing the impact of disability on a child's development. While services vary widely, they should be determined by the child's needs, not just what happens to be available. The document that spells out these needs and the services that will be provided to meet them is the Individual Family Service Plan (IFSP), a document based on an evaluation of your child that describes your child's level of functioning, goals, and the specific services that will be provided to meet his or her needs.

What an IEP Is

The document that spells out what your child's needs are and how they will be met after age three is the Individual Education Program (IEP). This document delineates your child's strengths and sets out objectives, and how these will be met within the school system.

Parents who challenge IEPs often end up in a due-process hearing with a "bipartisan" judge to determine if the school system is adhering to their obligations. If they are not, they may be found in violation. However, going this route is expensive and time-consuming for parents who are anxious to receive timely treatment for their children. Many due-process hearings favor the school board, and the process can demolish the relationship between the family and the school.

We ended up moving from one county to another rather than becoming embroiled in a long battle that would have left our children waiting on the sidelines.

What an FAPE Is

A basic legal right of every child is to have a free appropriate public education (FAPE). Even though your child is "entitled" to an

FAPE, the determination of what this means is not always straight-forward. A free appropriate public education does not necessarily mean best, only that your child will be provided an education deemed appropriate by school authorities, though it may not be considered adequate by you, the parents.

Depending on where you live, your child may be eligible for mandated services, but there may be no one in your area to provide them in a quality way.

What an LRE Is

Least restrictive environment (LRE) means a child should be placed in an environment in which he or she has the greatest op-portunity to participate in the general education curriculum and to interact with children who are not disabled.

If appropriate, a child with a disability should be mainstreamed into classes with students without disabilities. This can sometimes be accomplished with a trained one-on-one aide for assistance. In other cases, it may be considered more appropriate for a child to be placed in a special-education classroom, in a special-needs school, or in a home instruction program.

6. YOU MAY NEED TO EXIT MAINSTREAM MEDICINE TO FIND THE HELP YOU NEED

Conventional mainstream medicine may not have all the answers you're looking for, leaving you to search on your own for alterna-tive treatments to aid in your child's progress.

DAN! (Defeat Autism Now!) doctors, for example, stress a bio-medical approach to autism. They work with parents to utilize various treatments and supplements and cutting-edge therapies; their protocol encompasses intensive vitamin and mineral supple-mentation and a gluten-free diet.

In most cases, DAN! treatments are not covered by private medical insurances. Make sure you choose a DAN! doctor who is reputable and speak with other parents whose children have been treated by the doctor.

We found DAN! doctors much more open to individualizing treatments for each of our boys. Our DAN! doctors also actually *listened* to us as parents and looked past our sons' autism when they presented other medical symptoms. DAN! doctor visits can take hours in order to ensure a complete understanding of your child's medical status.

7. A CHANGE IN DIET—SUCH AS THE GLUTEN-FREE, CASEIN-FREE DIET—MAY HELP

What works for one child may not work for another, but a GFCF diet, which eliminates all wheat and dairy products, will not harm your child and may help. The GFCF diet is something you can try on your own at home; it may produce many beneficial effects, as it did for our boys.

Gluten and casein are common food allergens for those with autism. People with celiac disease use the gluten-free diet because their bodies can't process gluten, a protein in wheat and other grains, contained in a wide variety of foods such as bread and pasta. Casein is another common allergen found in all dairy products. Specialized markets and grocery stores now offer gluten-free pastas and other products.

A rule of thumb is to give any program or diet at least six months to see whether or not it is effective. We were amazed to see how one fairly simple dietary modification—the removal of dairy products—produced visible results in behavior and speech with all three of our boys.

This is a noninvasive intervention that parents can manage on their own, without side effects, though it may result in a heftier grocery bill.

8. NOT ALL MEDICAL INSURANCES ARE THE SAME, AND MANY THERAPIES AREN'T COVERED

Most medical insurance companies classify autism as a mental illness and refuse coverage for the prolonged, one-on-one therapies commonly prescribed for treating it.

ABA, AVB, Floortime, speech, physical therapy, occupational therapy, listening therapy, and sensory integration therapy are often NOT covered by the health insurance that is deducted from your paycheck by your employer. When there is coverage, most private insurance policies have service limitations, out-of-pocket expenses, and lifetime caps. Coverage also varies depending on whether your employer insurance is covered by ERISA, a federal law that sets minimum standards for most voluntarily established pension and health plans in private industry.

Even though Randy has a well-paying career, his health insurance would not pay for most of the treatments we have employed for our boys. We sold our home in order to move to a more progressive county that had autism programs comparable to the ones offered in private autism schools.

9. ALL STATES ARE NOT CREATED EQUAL IN QUALITY OR QUANTITY OF AUTISM SERVICES

There is no federally coordinated autism policy in the United States. This means that there is a hodgepodge of policy that varies from state to state. Maryland, for example, is one of only five states that provide Medicaid funding for autism services regardless of the family's income.

There is an income limit imposed on qualification for Supplemental Security Income (SSI) for children with disabilities. Some states, such as Georgia, have Deeming Waivers, once called Katie Beckett Waivers. These are a way for parents to obtain Medicaid for their disabled child when their income is too high to qualify for SSI. This federal waiver takes the family income out of the picture and looks at the income and assets of the child. Even if a child has private insurance coverage, parents can apply for this waiver.

As of 2007, only seventeen states afforded some level of coverage for autism-related services, according to a report from the Connecticut Office of Legislative Research. With a rise in the prevalence of autism among children in the country, there has a been a concerted effort by Autism Speaks and others to lobby each of the state legislatures to try to force the states to require private medical insurance companies to cover the therapies and treatments for autism.

10. YOUR CAREER PLANS MAY NEED TO BE ADJUSTED

Life will shift dramatically with an autism diagnosis. Your child's needs—educational, medical, and emotional—will move front and center. This in turn will have an impact on your career plans and working life; you may need to make adjustments as you find yourself confronted with perpetual appointments, consultations, and meetings. Many of these appointments will need to be scheduled during normal business hours, wreaking havoc on a nonflexible work schedule.

Some employers are compassionate and allow workers sabbaticals or flextime, or to work part-time from home. Other employers operate differently, and you may have to recalibrate your career goals.

We were lucky that Randy's employer allowed him to change his work hours so that he could help me with transportation, and to work from home when it was necessary. We were also fortunate that his job paid well enough that I could afford to quit my teaching job and stay at home to care for the boys.

11. CHILDREN *HAVE* BEEN VACCINE-INJURED

Despite years of government insistence to the contrary, it has now been firmly established that children *have* been injured by vaccines. There are many documented cases of parents who have been compensated by the federal vaccine court after a child has been vaccine-injured.

The National Vaccine Injury Compensation Program (VICP) has been established as a no-fault alternative to the traditional tort system for resolving vaccine injury claims. VICP provides compensation to people found to be injured by certain vaccines. For more information, go to: http://www.hrsa.gov/vaccinecompensation.

You can also report a child's reaction to a vaccine to the Vaccine Adverse Event Reporting System, a cooperative program for vaccine safety of the Centers for Disease Control and Prevention (CDC) and the Food and Drug Administration (FDA). VAERS collects information about adverse events (possible side effects) that occur after the administration of U.S.-licensed vaccines. Its website (http://vaers.hhs.gov/) provides a nationwide mechanism by which adverse events following immunization (AEFI) may be reported, analyzed, and made available to the public.

12. RESIST THE IMPULSE TO ISOLATE YOURSELF

Having a child with autism can be extremely isolating. When we first began our journey, we often felt completely alone. We kept to ourselves rather than spend time with people who didn't understand the disorder. There were few websites or support groups, and we didn't know any other families who were struggling with the same issues. Today, with more children being diagnosed than ever, there are numerous support groups, blogs, and websites.

Randy and I had no idea until our Autism Expo how many others were in our shoes. To hear another mother say, "Yes, our daughter was the same way, I know how you feel," brought a relief that was immense and immediate.

Make sure to connect with other families for sustenance, solace, and advice. You don't need to be alone.

13. PLAN FOR THE FUTURE

Parents of children with autism worry not just about the day but also about the future—how will a child be taken care of when they are no longer around? It is essential that you set up not just a will but a trust, if necessary, to address these vital concerns.

A special-needs trust (SNT) is one option for providing for an autistic child in the event of a parent's death. The SNT is designed to manage resources while maintaining the individual's eligibility for public assistance benefits. The family leaves whatever resources it considers appropriate to the trust. The trust is managed by a trustee on behalf of the person with the disability.

Although it may be sobering and disturbing to consider the fate of your child if you or your mate is no longer around, it is one of the hard tasks that Randy and I have come to terms with in our own future planning. Avoiding the topic won't make it go away.

Our children may need our guidance and financial assistance in the years to come, and we have made legal provisions that give us the peace of mind that they will have them.

14. ACCEPT THAT YOU WILL NEVER FEEL YOU'VE DONE ENOUGH

Even if you are doing everything humanly possible, you will always feel as if it's not enough—that you should be doing more for your child. Being an advocate for an autistic child is a full-time job and then some. It may feel overwhelming, but with perseverance and patience, you will find your way.

In our lives, we've often felt that as soon as we have one area of the boys' life under control—educational placement, for example—a health issue rears up, and we have to deal with that. Particularly in the case of three children, the different levels of needs and concerns seem infinite. One thing at a time, one day at a time, we get through.

15. YOUR CHILD *CAN* LEARN

No matter how young or old, children with autism are capable of learning. They need caregivers, teachers, and people who are engaging and supportive of them. Make sure whoever works with your child believes in his or her capabilities and knows that the sky is the limit.

As the gatekeeper of your child's treatment, you need to possess hope, grit, skepticism, and the ability to adapt. You have to be willing to continually change course; to try new interventions long enough to see whether they really work, then give up on them when they don't; to maneuver out of dead ends; and to hold your ground when others disagree with your deep instincts. And you have to remember that love and attention are as crucial to your child as any outside intervention you will ever locate.

16. TAKE CARE OF YOURSELF AND YOUR MARRIAGE

Anyone with an autistic child won't be surprised to learn that the divorce rate for parents of autistic children is a whopping 80 percent. In fact, it is sometimes listed as a common "side effect" of autism.

The chronic financial and emotional stresses involved in raising a special-needs child are real. When you place so much energy into the care of one family member, there is less time to dedicate to other relationships. But in order for your child to thrive, you need to remain healthy yourself and nurture your relationship as a couple.

In the early days of our boys' regression, Randy and I had some rough times. We were on different wavelengths, with me overwhelmed by the boys' symptoms and Randy desperately trying to explain them away. I often felt alone and desperate, second-guessing my own perceptions. Autism presents daily struggles that are compounded when you are working at cross-purposes or feel alienated from your spouse. We needed to unite and join forces for our family's survival, and luckily we did.

17. DO YOUR OWN RESEARCH

As the overseer and monitor of your child's treatment, therapy, and education, it's important that you do your own research. You are going to have to become a scientist, medical researcher, educational consultant, and legal wiz. You'll have to sift through tons of written material and surf through numerous sites on the Web.

If Randy and I hadn't been aware of the parameters and basics of ABA and AVB, for example, we wouldn't have been able to ascertain when a therapist was crossing boundaries, being too rough on the boys, or expecting too little. If we hadn't been conversant with special-education law in our state, we wouldn't have been able to demand the education and help our sons were entitled to.

The more that you know, the better equipped you will be to help your child succeed. Knowledge is power.

18. DEVELOP A THICK SKIN

There are still many people who don't understand what it means to have autism. You may receive withering looks when one of your kids has a meltdown in public—a look that speaks volumes: *Can't you control your child?*

You may receive a nasty glance of disapproval, as we did the other day, when you park in a disabled spot: *Your kids aren't disabled, why are you parking there?*

To the layperson, autism is often invisible; our sons don't appear any different from typical children. This is an attitude you'll encounter; just remember it's rooted in ignorance. Don't worry about the stares.

19. THE CAUSE OF AUTISM IS STILL CONTROVERSIAL

Parents have many passionately held beliefs about what caused their child's autism—from vaccinations to genetics. The topic haunts families and is fraught with emotion, controversy, guilt, and blame. However, autism is a complex disorder that defies a single causal theory. Most experts believe the disorder is caused by a combination of genetic and environmental factors, but no one has a definitive answer.

While we are uncertain ourselves what exactly precipitated our boys' condition, we try to respect other peoples' experiences and beliefs. The road of autism is difficult enough without families becoming alienated and angry because of differing views. We need to work together, not separate ourselves into opposing factions.

20. DO NOT GIVE UP

You will have to continually adapt and try new things in order to find out what works for your child. You will have to learn to be both persistent and patient. Your child will evolve in different ways over time.

New advances, research, and treatments are being introduced every year. Autism is a marathon, not a race. We try to keep a long and short view, making today as loving and fruitful as possible while keeping our hope alive for the future.

16

AUTISM THERAPIES AND
INTERVENTIONS

As the parents of triplets whose deficits virtually cover the full spectrum of autism, we have the distinction of being intimately involved, through both personal experience and intensive research, with available treatment programs. Since each of our boys has followed a separate trajectory, what has worked for one hasn't necessarily worked for the other.

Applied behavior analysis, applied verbal behavior, Floortime, TEACCH, and relationship development intervention are only a few of the popular programs available for families to consider. We've also tried and had success with less mainstream treatments, which we'll also address—for example the DAN! protocol, which encompasses the gluten-free, casein-free diet, intensive vitamin and mineral supplementation, and the controversial process of chelation.

In this chapter, we provide an easy-to-follow summation of

each treatment as well as our personal experiences with how various treatments have worked for our sons. We even include treatments that we take strong exception to, such as prescription drugs that are often prescribed for behavior and mood problems in youngsters with autism.

We believe that all parents have the right to choose the best treatment for their own child, but we also believe that this choice should be an informed one.

EDUCATIONAL INTERVENTIONS

Applied Behavior Analysis (ABA)

What It Is

Applied behavior analysis (ABA), the most widely recommended intervention, is a trial-and-reward system designed to wire connections in a child's brain that are impaired or missing because of autism. Dr. Ivar Lovaas developed the current model of ABA based on principles originally described by B. F. Skinner in the 1930s.

The main premise of ABA is that appropriate behavior can be taught using scientific principles and that children are more likely to repeat appropriate behaviors or responses that are rewarded and less likely to continue behaviors that are not reinforced.

Discrete trial teaching (DTT) is the best-known ABA technique, used in both traditional ABA and verbal behavior programs. The technique follows this protocol:

A. Break a new skill into smaller parts.
B. Teach one sub-skill at a time until mastered.
C. Provide intensive teaching.
D. Provide prompting and use prompt fading (gradually removing or reducing a prompt across learning trials until it is no longer provided) when appropriate.
E. Use reinforcement protocol.

Repetition and reinforcement are at the root of ABA, with skills broken down into small steps and with the child and therapist usually working together at a table. These components are then built upon so a child learns how to learn in a natural environment. The goal is to help children learn such skills as making eye contact, following simple instructions, imitating, using fine motor skills, and developing advanced social skills.

ABA focuses on the use of positive reinforcement to strengthen a behavior by arranging for it to be followed by something of value. This therapy stresses that receptive language needs to be developed before expressive language.

Discrete trials normally are one-on-one encounters, with the therapist or parent prompting the child to perform a specific action and rewarding success with positive reinforcement, based on the ABC model:

A—ANTECEDENT

A request or directive, asking the child to perform an action.

B—BEHAVIOR

A behavior or response from the child—successful performance, noncompliance, or no response.

C—CONSEQUENCE

A consequence, defined as the reaction from the therapist. This may range from strong positive reinforcement, such as praise or a treat, to a strong negative response.

The aim of ABA is to alter the way the child responds to things so that he learns how to learn like his typically developing peers. Starting with general compliance, common goals include sitting down in a chair, listening to a story, imitating single sounds, or completing a puzzle.

Pros: ABA is generally considered the most effective and rigorously tested intervention for children on the autistic spectrum, with the potential to help children gain the skills they need to overcome their disorder.

Cons: Repetitive and regimented, ABA can sometimes lead to rote and robotlike behaviors in children. The therapy is also expensive and is often not paid for by health insurance or the school system and requires a therapist who possesses a high degree of skill.

A therapist without the necessary experience or expertise could actually hamper a child's development. Because of this, it's important to check an ABA therapist's credentials, including a résumé with work experience, college training, and references. Also make sure your program is being overseen by a BCBA (board-certified behavioral analyst) and/or a licensed psychologist.

Our Experience

We found Lovaas-style ABA too repetitive and excessively regimented, particularly for Nicholas and Hunter, who did not respond well to the negative reinforcements. They could not comprehend why they were being told "No" when they got a wrong answer or inserted an incorrect puzzle piece. Nicholas learned a few skills through this method, but they seemed robotic and unnatural. And Hunter had no interest in putting a puzzle together or remaining seated at a table while he did so.

Lovaas-style ABA worked best for Zachary, who already possessed receptive language skills and a higher level of hierarchical skills than those of Nicholas and Hunter. He understood what he was being asked to do and didn't view the request negatively. He is considered by the school system a mainstreamed child, since his developmental disability does not impair his ability to learn with his neurotypical peers. His social awareness is a little off, but for the most part he blends in and performs well academically.

Implementing ABA also involved a weekly hourlong meeting with the psychologist overseeing each boy's program along with the lead teacher and technicians. During this meeting, we would all observe the tasks the boys were working on, and the psychologist would offer guidance on methods that might increase the boys' success.

Applied Verbal Behavior Intervention (AVB)

WHAT IT IS

Applied verbal behavior focuses on expressive language and aims to make language functional for a child with autism. If a child wants something—say, a cookie—AVB helps him find a way to communicate this by any means possible—vocally or through sign language or picture exchange communication.

AVB utilizes B. F. Skinner's analysis of verbal behavior to elicit and reinforce speech. A verbal behavior program focuses on making a child realize that language will get him what he wants, when he wants it.

AVB focuses on three primary verbal operants: mands, tacts, and intraverbals.

MANDS

The most important part of any verbal behavior program is to get the child to request things that he or she desires—a process called manding. Every mand is an opportunity for the child to engage with the therapist and also to learn that language has a purpose and will get him what he wants.

For example, the child learns to say "candy bar" when he is interested in obtaining a candy bar. When he is given the candy bar, the words are reinforced; they will be used again in the same context, thus emphasizing the "function" of language.

Tacts

A tact is a form of labeling language that communicates what a child sees, hears, tastes, and smells. Tacting requires coming up with correct words and pronouncing them correctly. A child might say "candy bar" when seeing a picture of one, thus labeling it. Tacting involves the child as a speaker, not as a listener.

Intraverbals

Intraverbals are to-and-from conversational exchanges that include filling in the blanks, finishing song lines, or answering questions. They allow a child to speak about objects and events even though they are not present, a feature of conversational language.

Intraverbals are responses to the language of another person, usually answers to "wh-" questions. If you say to the child "I'm baking . . ." and the child finishes the sentence with "cookies," that's an intraverbal fill-in.

Pros: AVB attempts to capture the motivation of a child to develop a connection between the value of a word and the word itself. With AVB, our sons would find a way to ask for a cookie— through sign, or filling in a blank—because *they wanted one.*

Cons: Like ABA, AVB is an expensive treatment that is often not paid for by health insurance or school systems.

Our Experience

Our primary goal was to encourage speech in our boys, and applied verbal behavior has been a wonderful way to teach them about language. There are no negative reinforcers used in AVB, only positive ones. The boys have responded well to AVB's heavy reliance on eliciting the child's participation and willingness to communicate wants and needs verbally or nonverbally.

Hunter and Nicholas especially thrived in this environment. Hunter lit up while working with his therapist and began speaking in one-word snippets, while Nicholas laughed with delight as if he couldn't believe he'd finally found someone who understood him unconditionally. Both boys would mand up a storm to get their teacher to sing or play with them.

We also found it was beneficial for the boys to work in their natural environment, away from a table, and to be allowed to act as they do when the therapists aren't there. Since there is no wrong answer, they discovered that learning can be fun.

Floortime

What It Is

Floortime is a treatment method developed by child psychiatrist Stanley Greenspan that is centered on interactive play and relationship. The treatment is called Floortime because a parent is urged to get down on the floor and engage with the child at his level, enter the child's activities, and follows the child's lead in order to help him develop interaction and communication skills. The parent is shown how to move the child toward increasingly more complex interactions, a process known as "opening and closing circles of communication."

Floortime is based on the belief that development consists of a ladder of milestones that children climb, one rung at a time, in sequence. The goal is to move the child through the emotional and developmental milestones that must be mastered for emotional and intellectual growth.

Greenspan describes these developmental milestones as:

1. Self-regulation and interest in the world
2. Intimacy or a special love for the world of human relations
3. Two-way communication
4. Complex communication
5. Emotional ideas
6. Emotional thinking

Pros: Floortime takes place in the natural home environment and allows a parent to become a child again—getting down on the floor and spending time engaging a child, following his lead. Parents don't dominate in this therapy, but are in an equal partnership with the child.

There is no negative response in Floortime. As a stepping stone, we found it to be the least intrusive and most natural therapy, one that could be applied throughout the day.

Cons: Floortime can be difficult to facilitate for the daily six twenty-minute sessions that are necessary in order to be effective. While school systems may incorporate this strategy into their programs, generally they do not make this their primary means of educating young children with autism. This therapy is not commonly paid for by health insurance.

Our Experience

Floortime was the first therapy we used, and we chose it because we could use it ourselves at home. This approach worked for all three of our boys.

We were able to get the boys to ask us verbally or through gestures for familiar things by hiding their favorite toys or objects and keeping them engaged at all times, even if the communication circles were nonverbal.

For example, if Zachary was playing with his Thomas the Tank Engine train, we would play along with him and try to get him to engage with us and communicate what he was trying to do. Instead of simply lining up the trains, we would make up scenarios about where the trains were going. Sometimes we would hide Thomas under a pillow or blanket and ask, "Where's Thomas?" and get Zachary engaged in searching for the train. Eventually, Zachary would also ask, "Where's Thomas?" thus bridging what we'd taught him—how to interact with us instead of remaining inside himself.

If Hunter were flapping his arms and we couldn't get him to engage with us, we would follow his lead and flap along, pretending we were an airplane. Our goal was to distract him from his own movements, to get him to pay attention and engage with us, and to make the action of arm-flapping seem more purposeful to him.

Our main Floortime goal was to get the boys to ask through interaction for favorite things for about twenty minutes, six times a day. The system was circular. Each exchange back and forth was considered one full circle. The goal was to get many exchanges back and forth in order to increase the social interaction and bring the child out from within.

Relationship Development Intervention (RDI)

WHAT IT IS

Relationship development intervention (RDI) is a parent-based treatment based on the work of psychologist Steven Gutstein. RDI is based on the belief that relationships are central to the quality of a person's life. The goal of RDI is to help children with autism develop mental and emotional flexibility, curiosity, self-assurance and empathy so that they can form relationships out in the world. The treatment focuses on the core issues of gaining friendships, feeling empathy, expressing love, and learning to share experiences with others.

RDI is a parent-led approach where the child learns to trust the parent and then follows his/her lead. It aims to cultivate the building blocks of social connection that normally develop in infancy and early childhood. These include the following six aspects:

1. Emotional referencing: The ability to use an emotional feedback system to learn from the subjective experiences of others.
2. Social coordination: The ability to observe and continually regulate one's behavior in order to participate in spontaneous relationships involving collaboration and exchange of emotions.
3. Declarative language: Using language and nonverbal

communication to express curiosity, invite others to interact, share perceptions and feelings, and coordinate actions with others.

4. Flexible thinking: The ability to adapt, change strategies, and alter plans based upon changing circumstances.

5. Relational information processing: The ability to obtain meaning based upon a larger context. Solving problems that have no "right" or "wrong" solutions.

6. Foresight and hindsight: The ability to reflect on past experiences and anticipate potential future scenarios in a productive manner.

Often directly marketed to parents, the program offers training workshops for parents, as well as books with step-by step exercises. It encourages the incorporation of your child into your daily routine, utilizing simple tasks such as doing laundry or planting a garden together, which can become opportunities for teaching the child how to work cooperatively.

Pros: The program claims to be started easily and implemented into regular, daily activities that enrich family life.

Gutstein is an advocate of balance and an opponent of over-treatment of children with autism. He believes that the brain remains flexible throughout life and that parents needn't put additional pressure on themselves to recover their kids during the early years only.

Cons: RDI involves reframing the interactions between parent and child, and modifying the home environment. This may be more work than a parent wants to do.

The RDI "protocol," as outlined by Gutstein's Connections Center, includes a four-day parent workshop, an intensive initial assessment, and ongoing work with a certified RDI consultant; it's expensive and not paid for by health insurance.

TEACCH

WHAT IT IS

The TEACCH approach (Treatment and Education of Autistic and Related Communication Handicapped Children) is a special education program developed at the University of North Carolina that has been adopted by many school and educational systems in order to teach academic skills and address the needs of children with varying degrees of autism. The method focuses on the design of the physical, social, and communicating environment, which is structured to accommodate the difficulties of children with autism while it trains them to perform in acceptable and appropriate ways.

TEACCH originated in the 1960s when doctors Eric Schopler, R. J. Reichler, and Margaret Lansing constructed a means to gain control of a teaching setup so that independence could be fostered in children.

A TEACCH classroom is usually a highly structured environment with clearly delineated activity areas for such tasks as individual work, group activities, and play. This is based on the belief that structure for autistic children provides a strong base and framework for learning.

TEACCH relies heavily on visual learning, with children using schedules made up of pictures or words to order their day and to help guide them smoothly between activities. Children learn how to complete a number of tasks, thus promoting independent work skills.

Pros: TEACCH relies heavily on visual learning, which is a strength for many children with autism.

Cons: Since TEACCH is more focused on accommodating a child's autistic traits than on trying to overcome them, social interaction and verbal communication are not usually heavily stressed.

There has been criticism that TEACCH is too rigid and geared toward routine and a need for predictability.

OUR EXPERIENCE

The boys went to a special-needs preschool that used TEACCH for a year, but we found that it was not a successful approach for them. This method seemed too rigid for the boys and didn't focus on the one thing that they needed the most help with—verbal communication. Because the method wasn't language centered and didn't follow the boys' motivation or lead, they were bored and unmotivated.

The Son-Rise Program

WHAT IT IS

Son-Rise is a child-centered, home-based approach that focuses on interaction, language, and relationships. The program originated in 1974 with two parents, Barry Neil Kaufman and Samahria Lyte Kaufman, who claimed to have "cured" their autistic son, Raun, and then proceeded to write a book about it called *Son-Rise: The Miracle Continues*. They also founded the Option Institute and Fellowship in Sheffield, Massachusetts. The institute offers training for families wishing to create home-based Son-Rise Programs for their children.

The program is geared toward building the self-esteem of children with autism and helping them trust and enjoy other people and their environment. As part of its strategy, it uses relationships to assist autistic children in managing their difficulties. The starting point is acceptance of the child's world. A parent is encouraged to join in with a child's ritualistic behaviors, which is believed to facilitate eye contact, play, and social interaction. Generally a parent is encouraged to teach through interactive play in order to encourage meaningful social communication.

Son-Rise utilizes the home as a nurturing environment in which to help children. A separate room with a blank wall, a few toys, and large mirrors is recommended for this therapy. The room provides little stimulation; the only stimulation the child will receive is from the parent.

Pros: Family-centered, can be done at home.

Cons: No formal studies or evaluations have validated the effectiveness of the Son-Rise Program as a treatment for children with autism. This program is expensive and not covered by health insurance.

OCCUPATIONAL THERAPY

Sensory Integration Therapy (SIT)

WHAT IT IS

A sensory integration program is specifically tailored to a child with autism in order to provide sensory stimulation, often in conjunction with purposeful muscle activities, to improve how the brain processes sensory information.

Children with autism may have atypical responses to sounds, sights, physical sensations, smells, or movements. Because they seem underresponsive or overresponsive to sensory stimuli, they may be suspected of being deaf or visually impaired and referred for hearing and vision tests.

Autistic children often have mild, moderate, or severe sensory integration dysfunction, or SID. SID deficits manifest in either increased sensitivity (hypersensitivity) or decreased sensitivity (hyposensitivity) to touch, sound, and movement. A hypersensitive child may shy away from being touched, whereas a hyposensitive child will seek the stimulation of feeling objects. The feel of certain fabrics, the taste of particular foods, or everyday sounds may precipitate emotional outbursts. Conversely, an autistic child may feel little pain or enjoy strong smells, intense cold, or unpleasant tastes.

Often the child exhibits difficulties in movement, coordination, and sensing where his or her body is in a given space. In these cases, the brain is unable to filter out background stimuli and admit what is important. Because of this the child with autism has to regularly contend with overwhelming amounts of sensory input.

Evaluation and treatment of basic sensory integrative processes are most commonly performed by an occupational and/or physical therapist. The usual form of SIT is a type of occupational therapy that places a child in a room specifically designed to stimulate and challenge all of the senses. The therapist works closely with the child to encourage movement within the room.

The therapy often requires activities that consist of full body movements utilizing different types of equipment. While SIT does not teach higher-level skills, it enhances sensory processing abilities, thus allowing the child to acquire them, and helps children process the information they receive from their senses in a more typical manner.

Pros: Children with autism may qualify for free physical and occupational therapy at their schools or through early intervention programs. Also, parents and caregivers can learn sensory activities to perform with a child at home.

Cons: This therapy can be expensive if not covered by insurance or provided by the school or early intervention programs.

OUR EXPERIENCE

We've successfully utilized private occupational therapy and the boys have also received this therapy in school. The boys have a "sensory plan" or "sensory diet" that is incorporated into their school day, as follows:

Zachary's Sensory Plan

This plan is designed to help Zachary achieve his maximum learning potential through either calming activities or alerting activities that help him attain and maintain appropriate levels of attention in the classroom and to reduce self-stimulatory behaviors during classroom activities.

Environmental Modifications

Allow Zachary to sit in a quiet area when appropriate to decrease distraction. Allow him to stand if he needs to or take short walks within the classroom upon completion of activities.

Reduce visual distractions by turning the lights down, allowing him to work where he's not distracted by peers who may be talking or playing.

Reduce auditory distractions by providing a quiet area and soft background music.

Provide a quiet corner, which Zachary may need in times of stress. Provide a beanbag chair and soft pillows in order to provide deep calming pressure and reduced visual and auditory stimulation.

During recess, encourage Zachary to run, climb, and swing in order to obtain organizing and alerting sensory input in the natural context of an activity.

Zachary also needs at least one sensory break per hour because of his acute sensory needs.

Nicholas and Hunter's Sensory Plans

Guidelines for activities that will help keep the boys calm and ready for learning:

For vestibular system: Use various swings primarily with linear movement. Bounce on balls, take wagon rides, play on the playground, use the mini trampoline and rocking chair, and ride a bike.

For proprioceptive system, which gives information about where body parts are in space and in relation to one another and where sensory receptors are in the muscles, joints, and skin: Provide chewy tube for deep pressure in the jaw. Nicholas and Hunter can also try to push or pull items, such as pushing the pedals of a bike or pulling a weighted cart.

Drinking from a straw also helpful. Playing catch with a weighted ball also helpful.

For smell, allow Nicholas and Hunter to use a "smell box" with different scents, which also could be used as a reinforcer.

COMMUNICATION INTERVENTIONS

PECS (Picture Exchange Communication System)

What It Is

PECS is an augmentative and alternative communication system that is generally utilized as an aid for nonverbal children with autism. With PECS, children learn to communicate using picture cards.

PECS are typically introduced by teaching a child to exchange a picture of a desired item with a communicative partner who immediately honors the request (considered a mand within B. F. Skinner terminology). These pictures can be hand-drawn illustrations, photos, or computer clip art printed on sheets of paper.

When the child wants one of these items, he gives the picture to a parent, therapist, caregiver, or another child. The communication partner then hands the child the food or toy, thus reinforcing communication. Ultimately, the pictures can be replaced with words and sentence strips (for example, "I want candy").

PECS typically moves through six stages:

- Teaching a child to spontaneously request an object or activity.
- Generalizing this skill to other objects, activities, and people
- Teaching the child to discriminate—"What would you like to do?"
- Encouraging the use of sentences—for example, using the symbols for "I want" and "the ball."
- Extending sentences with an adjective such as "I want the *blue* ball."
- Encouraging the child to comment on things—for instance using symbols to say "I can smell dinner cooking."

PECS thus starts with a basic request and eventually forms the basis for conversation, which provides an ideal foundation for verbal skills at a later point.

Pros: For a family with a nonverbal child who is not grasping sign language, PECS can be a great aid to communication. By providing a communication outlet, it can help nonverbal children to be less frustrated.

PECS protocols and teaching strategies have been scientifically validated within the field of applied behavior analysis.

Cons: The introduction of PECS can be a time-consuming process taking months to complete, depending on your child's response. You must also carry your child's PEC book everywhere you go. There is not always a picture for everything.

Our Experience

PECS has been very useful for our boys, especially Nicholas, our least verbal son, who responded dramatically to this method. If a child doesn't possess the fine motor skills needed to utilize sign language, PECS is a good alternative. It can also help with a verbal child who can't think of a word quickly enough or with augmenting communication.

Speech Therapy

What It Is

A speech therapist working with an autistic child or adult may work on a wide range of skills, including:

- Nonverbal communication, entailing gestures, picture exchange cards, electronic talking devices, and so on

- Speech pragmatics: how and to whom particular speech is appropriate
- Conversation skills, including "joint attention," a back-and-forth exchange. This involves eye gaze and such gesturing as pointing, showing, or giving.

Speech therapy is often recommended for those diagnosed on the autism spectrum, whether they are nonverbal or extremely verbal. People with autism often exhibit difficulties in the practical application of language and are likely to misuse and misunderstand language.

Some children exhibit echolalia, or repeating verbatim what they've heard; others speak words that convey little information; others use robotlike speech.

Pros: Because speech-language therapy is well established, it is likely that medical insurance may cover at least part of the cost. School and early intervention providers are also likely to provide speech therapy.

Our Experience

Working within the classroom, a speech therapist is able to incorporate therapy right into the boys' daily schedule without their even being aware of it. For example, the SLP often uses lunchtime to work with the boys, sitting down and eating with them and having them request food items using their PECS books. In this way she gains their trust and attention, and their therapy becomes a natural component of their daily routine.

We have found speech therapy helpful as long as the therapist is adequately trained in how to engage and work effectively with a child who has autism.

BIOMEDICAL TREATMENTS

Medical, Dietary, and Supplement Interventions

Parents are often overwhelmed by the scores of potential medical and dietary interventions and the competing theories embodied by them. One recent study by Dr. Vanessa Green and her colleagues at the University of Texas at Austin found that more than one hundred different treatments were being tried by families across the United States. Parents, on average, were using *seven different treatments* at one time for their child. Many of even the most commonly used treatments lack empirical support.

We have cycled through many of these therapies ourselves. We include here the most common and well documented of these interventions, and comment on the ones that have worked for us.

MEDICAL INTERVENTIONS

Prescription medications cannot cure autism, but they may be prescribed to treat specific symptoms.

Children suffering from autism often exhibit a wide variety of different symptoms; these include not only behavioral, social, and sensory but also physical symptoms, such as gastrointestinal problems and seizures.

Common autism symptoms that are often treated with prescription drugs include behavioral problems, depression and anxiety, obsessive-compulsive disorder, attention problems, and hyperactivity.

All pharmaceuticals present risks and the potential for side effects.

Behavioral Problems

Antipsychotics may be prescribed when behavioral symptoms, such as aggression, temper tantrums, or self-injury, become dangerous or out of control.

Risperdal (risperidone) is an antipsychotic medication that was FDA-approved in 2006 for the symptomatic treatment of irritability in autistic children and adolescents ages five to sixteen. The approval is the first for the use of a drug to treat behaviors associated with autism in children. Common side effects are increased appetite, weight gain, and sedation. Further long-term studies are needed to determine any long-term side effects.

Other atypical antipsychotics that have been studied with encouraging results are olanzapine (Zyprexa) and ziprasidone (Geodon). Olanzapine (Zyprexa) and other antipsychotic medications are often used off-label for the treatment of aggression and other serious behavioral disturbances in children with autism. This means a doctor will prescribe a medication to treat a disorder or to use in an age group that is not included among those approved by the FDA.

While older antipsychotics such as haloperidol, thioridazine, fluphenazine, and chlorpromazine may be effective for treating behavioral problems, they may present serious side effects, such as abnormal movements, muscle stiffness, and sedation.

Depression and Anxiety

Selective serotonin reuptake inhibitors (SSRIs) are prescribed for anxiety, depression, and obsessive-compulsive disorder in children with autism. Prozac is the only one of these drugs that has been approved for both depression and OCD in children age seven and older. Zoloft is also approved for children age seven and older with OCD, Luvox for children eight and older, and Anafranil for those ten and older.

In 2004, the FDA adopted a "black box" warning label on all antidepressant medications to alert the public about the potential increased risk of suicidal thinking or attempts in children and adolescents taking antidepressants. In 2007, the agency extended the warning to include young adults up to age twenty-five. A black-box warning is the most serious type of warning on prescription drug labeling. The warning emphasizes that children, adolescents, and young adults taking antidepressants should be closely monitored, especially during the initial weeks of treatment, for any worsening depression, suicidal thinking or behavior, or any unusual changes in behavior such as sleeplessness, agitation, or withdrawal from normal social situations.

Hyperactivity and Inattention

Ritalin and Concerta are two stimulant medications, commonly used to treat attention deficit hyperactivity disorder, which have also been prescribed for children with autism. They are prescribed in order to decrease hyperactivity and impulsivity, especially in higher-functioning children. Adderall, another stimulant, is also used to help with focus and attention issues.

Side effects for these drugs include irritability, reduced appetite, rebound, sleeplessness, seizures, repetitive movements, and increased blood pressure.

Opiate blockers are a type of drug that blocks the effects of natural opiates in the system. This makes some people, including those with autism, seem more responsive to their environment. These drugs, such as naltrexone (ReVia) also may control self-injurious behaviors.

Seizures

Seizures are common in autism. Some research estimates that up to 30 percent of autistic persons develop them. Seizure disorders are commonly treated with such anticonvulsants as carbamazepine (Tegretol), lamotrigine (Lamictal), topiramate (Topamax), and valproic acid (Depakote). Blood levels of the medication must be carefully monitored and adjusted so that the least amount possible is used to be effective.

OUR EXPERIENCE

We personally do not use these types of prescription drugs for our boys and would never use them. Many of them are used "off label";

in other words, they were not approved expressly for autism but for another ailment. And many of them have not been in use long enough for their side effects to be evident, especially in developing children.

We are fortunate that our boys don't currently have any severe behavioral problems or self-injurious behaviors that might warrant medication; we have great understanding and appreciation for families who end up putting their children on medications to keep them from harming themselves and others.

But given the lack of long-term research, and the possibility of serious side effects, we believe that we need to find the underlying cause of these severe behaviors to help reduce the likelihood of recurrence. We know families whose children were placed on these medications and then gained astronomical amounts of weight— one hundred pounds in one case—with no behavioral improvement. In some cases there was even a deterioration in behavior, to which the doctor responded by prescribing a newer medication, thereby creating a pharmaceutical merry-go-round.

If our sons ever developed severe behavioral issues, we would look to prescription drugs as a last resort and only after we turned over every stone possible, including moving to a home in the country and homeschooling the boys. However, we also believe that parents must do what they believe is best for their own children. If you think your child needs medication, discuss all side effects and long-term problems with your doctor.

DIET AND SUPPLEMENTS

DAN! (Defeat Autism Now!)

The DAN! (Defeat Autism Now!) protocol is a biomedical approach to autism treatment that combines eliminating dairy, cereal, and refined sugars with an intensive vitamin and mineral supplementation. DAN! doctors believe that autism is a disorder caused by a combination of lowered immune response, external toxins from vaccines and other sources, and problems caused by certain foods.

The DAN! philosophy involves trying to treat the underlying causes of the symptoms of autism, based on medical testing, scientific research, and clinical experience, with an emphasis on nutritional interventions. Many of the DAN! treatments have been found by listening to parents and physicians.

Some major interventions suggested by DAN! practitioners include:

- Nutritional supplements, including vitamins, minerals, amino acids, and essential fatty acids
- Special diets free of gluten and dairy products
- Testing for hidden food allergies and avoidance of allergenic foods
- Treatment of intestinal bacteria and yeast overgrowth with probiotics, supplements, and other nonpharmaceutical medications
- Detoxification of heavy metals through chelation (a potentially hazardous medical procedure)

Not all DAN! doctors are credentialed physicians; some practitioners are naturopaths, homeopaths, and nutritionists.

OUR EXPERIENCE

On our first encounter with a DAN! doctor, supplements such as cod liver oil and probiotics were prescribed based on the boys' urine and blood test results. Children with autism often have gastrointestinal problems and possess low levels of beneficial gut bacteria. These bacteria assist in food digestion and help limit the growth of harmful bacteria and yeast, which can affect behavior and mental functioning.

Probiotics, a combination of one or more beneficial bacteria, along with an antifungal diet low on yeast products, fruit juice, cheese, and mushrooms, can help restore normal gut function.

We've personally used *Lactobacillus acidophilus*, a safe, gut-friendly bacterium that aids in cleaning out the lower intestines and protects the body against harmful bacteria. Our initial experience with the protocol was positive, with the boys showing improvement.

Later we visited another DAN! practitioner when Hunter was diagnosed with a vitamin D deficiency and began experiencing pain and muscle spasms. The DAN! doctor prescribed vitamin D_3, which has been very helpful in helping with Hunter's muscle spasms. He was prescribed a list of supplements and has responded well.

The boys have also taken melatonin for sleep problems. Children with autism often have difficulty with sleep, from falling asleep, to staying asleep, to early waking. Melatonin is a hormone naturally produced in the brain by the pineal gland. The synthesis and release of melatonin are stimulated by darkness and suppressed by light. Levels of melatonin in the blood are highest prior to bedtime.

We've also used dye-free Benadryl, as suggested by our physician. It may cause excitability in some children, however.

All of the boys take the following:

Epsom salt baths
Quercetin
Magnesium
GABA
Vitamin D$_3$
Probiotics
Cod liver oil
Omega-3's
Enzymes
Coromega
Zinc

Gluten-Free, Casein-Free Diet
A GFCF diet involves avoidance of gluten and dairy products. Gastrointestinal problems are common in children with autism. These can be caused by an immature digestive system that is unable to break down complex protein found in wheat (gluten) or dairy (casein). Symptoms, some of which your child may not be

able to communicate, include constipation, diarrhea, vomiting, reflux, abdominal pain, heartburn, and bloated belly.

Gluten and casein allergies are common in those with autism. Wheat, barley, rye, and oats all contain gluten as do bread and pasta. Casein is found in all dairy products, including milk, yogurt, cheese, ice cream, salad dressing, nutritional bars, chocolate, lactose-free foods, and some multivitamins. Peptides in these foods have a potent effect on the brain and can result in such problems as aggression, self-abusive behavior, sleepiness, and inattention.

Some children also benefit from the removal of soy and/or corn products from their diet. Benefits usually are visible within several months.

If a casein-free diet is used, a calcium supplement should be given.

OUR EXPERIENCE

We try to follow a GFCF diet and have seen a marked difference in our boys' behaviors and some speech simply by removing dairy from their diets. We also try to avoid giving the boys artificially colored foods and to provide them with as much organic food as possible.

The only downside of the diet from our perspective is the high cost of the specialized foods and the need to shop at special markets.

Specific Carbohydrate Diet (SCD)

SCD is based on the theory that starches and certain sugars feed bacteria, yeast, and fungi—harmful microbes that cause GI problems, autism, and other illnesses. The SCD diet eliminates these microbes, and the gut/brain connection is repaired. The SCD diet contains no sugar or starch and is gluten free. Any dairy must be lactose free and contain denatured casein.

Vitamin Therapy

Many parents report success with megavitamin therapy. A number of studies have shown that vitamin B_6 combined with magnesium helps improve eye contact and speech, and lessens tantrums in children with autism. Studies have also shown this vitamin may help control hyperactivity and improve overall behavior. Other possible improvements include: better speech, healthier sleeping patterns, less irritability, longer attention span, less self-stimulation, and better general health.

Vitamin B_6–magnesium causes fewer side effects than other medications and is considered safe when used in appropriate doses. Dimethylglycine (DMG) is a food substance found in small amounts in brown rice and liver. This compound, available in many health food stores, is legally classified as a food. Some researchers claim that it improves speech in children with autism, along with eye contact, social behavior, and attention span. Those who respond to this treatment will usually do so within a week.

Essential Fatty Acids

The levels of two essential fatty acids, omega-3 and omega-6, both found in fish, are low throughout the population and are implicated in a wide range of disorders, including depression and bipolar disorder.

Children with autism have been found to possess levels of omega-3 fatty acids lower than those of typical children. Research has suggested that fatty-acid supplementation may increase language and learning skills in children with autism.

Since many fish are also high in mercury and other toxins, it may be safer for children to obtain fatty acids from fish oil supplements, which should be refrigerated.

Our Experience

We've had good luck with SuperNuThera and omega supplementation. Within days of giving these supplements to the boys, their language seemed to increase and their attention improved.

ALTERNATIVE THERAPIES

Animal-Assisted Therapy (AAT)

What It Is

Animal-assisted therapy (AAT) pairs specially trained therapy dogs with children with autism to increase social interaction and improve speech. The therapy is rapidly becoming a powerful tool at the disposal of trained professionals. Dogs have also been specially trained as safety companions for autistic children.

Studies of animal therapy have shown that exposure to animals helps improve morale and communication, bolster self-esteem, calm anxiety, and even reduce blood pressure and heart rate. Specific animal therapies can augment traditional physical, occupational, or even speech therapy. Animals used in therapy help children, even those with severe challenges, to feel better about themselves.

Our Experience

We have no personal experience with this therapy, but we think it is a wonderful idea.

One of my deepest fears about the boys being in school is that one of them will elope—simply take off on his own or with a stranger—and be unable to communicate who he is. A dog trained to stay by a child's side greatly minimizes this danger, which is reason enough to recommend this therapy.

Chelation

Subcribing to the belief that heavy-metal poisoning may trigger the symptoms of autism, some parents have turned to alternative-medicine practitioners who provide chelation therapy, which was originally used for treating lead poisoning.

Chelation is a process that involves ridding the body of metals, including mercury. In its most aggressive form, it is performed intravenously, but most parents give their autistic children a milder oral medication or a cream that is absorbed through the skin. The chelation agent binds to the mercury, which is then passed through the system.

Chelation therapy is not approved as an autism treatment and is still considered controversial. It has also been associated with serious side effects, including liver and kidney damage that can result in death.

Hyperbaric Oxygen Therapy (HBOT)

Hyperbaric Oxygen Therapy (HBOT) has received attention as a possible treatment for autism. This is the treatment used to cure scuba divers who suffer from the "bends"—a disorder that is the result of surfacing too quickly and thereby causing formation of nitrogen bubbles in the bloodstream.

A hyperbaric chamber is a pressurized, oxygen-filled chamber or tube that forces large quantities of oxygen into the body very quickly. Medical researchers have discovered a number of additional therapeutic uses for the chambers: It can speed the development of blood vessels, improving outcomes for certain types of wounds, gangrene, cardiac illnesses, and other conditions.

Some researchers have theorized that HBOT can improve symptoms of autism by increasing oxygen intake and thus reducing inflammation and hypoperfusion (lack of oxygen) in the brain. However, there is no consensus within the scientific community that inflammation or lack of oxygen cause autism or are even generally associated with autism.

Despite the lack of scientific evidence for HBOT as an effective autism treatment, HBOT clinics have been set up to provide treatment and "home" oxygen chambers. Expensive courses of HBOT treatment are being offered by various practitioners.

There are reported risks of side effects when using HBOT, including ear pain, reversible nearsightedness, and seizures.

Neurofeedback

WHAT IT IS

Neurofeedback is a noninvasive training that is similar to biofeedback used by athletes to boost performance. Neurofeedback aims to retrain the brain, based on the principle that the brain is a flexible, adaptable organ that can change with assistance from directed stimuli such as light, movement, and sound. Neurofeedback exercises, calms, and strengthens the brain and improves its stability.

Electrodes are applied to the scalp to monitor brainwave activity. The process is signaled by computer, and information is extracted about certain key brainwave frequencies. The ebb and flow of this activity is shown to the child, who attempts to change the activity level. Some frequencies are to be promoted; others diminished. This is presented to the child in the form of a video game. The child is effectively playing the video game with his brain. Brainwave activity is eventually shaped toward more desirable and regulated performance.

The claim is that the brain is creating new pathways in response to neurofeedback. As the brain is continually used, it maintains this new skill. In the case of autism, the training is aimed at organizing the brain to function better.

This therapy is typically provided by mental health professionals such as psychologists, family therapists, and counselors.

Pros: Painless, works with no side effects, and is less expensive than drugs.

Cons: Insurance companies usually do not pay for neurofeedback, and it requires a significant time commitment (up to three or four times a week in the beginning). While some researchers suggest that neurofeedback has produced good results for children with autism, there have not been rigorous clinical trials on this treatment.

AFTERWORD

As we finish writing this book, we have just returned from taking our boys to their first day at a new elementary school with unfamiliar teachers and a different building—a major change in their lives and ours.

Our relief at finding the perfect setting for them after our move to the new county was short-lived; unfortunately, they were in the last year of their early intervention period and by the end of the year their elementary school placement had to be decided. The pilot program that the boys had thrived in during kindergarten was now going to be located in a local elementary school, and Nicholas and Hunter were to be transferred directly there. Called Primary Learners, the class contains a total of only five boys, and each of them has an aide.

To our initial delight, because Zachary's kindergarten teacher noted he was so high-achieving, it was decided that he could be mainstreamed into a regular first-grade classroom, apart from his brothers but in the same building.

I say initial delight, because of what happened when Randy and I took the boys to school today.

As we got nearer to the school, I had a sense of foreboding similar to the one I had had at the preschool that was such a disaster a few years ago. As soon as we pulled up in front of the building, my radar was on full alert. The impatient lady directing traffic expected our sons to jump out of their car seats and head directly in to find their classrooms on their own.

"C'mon, c'mon," she called, until we told her that we were bypassing the normal parking lot because we were meeting up with the boys' chaperones—their autism valets—for the day. Besides, there was no way we were going to simply dump them off like a pile of laundry. This morning was going to be hard on all of us. It was going to be as difficult for the boys to separate from us and walk into an unfamiliar world of total strangers as it was for us leave them.

When we walked through the side door, I couldn't help noticing that the boys were dragging their feet, looking up at us anxiously as the moment drew near. As their aides appeared, Randy said, "Okay, boys, give us a kiss. Nicholas and Hunter, your aide is right there to take you to class. And Zach, yours is right here."

They dutifully kissed us, adjusted their book bags, and walked away with a reluctant bravery that made tears fill my eyes.

We stood watching Nicholas and Hunter shuffle forward reluctantly into a sea of unfamiliar faces. But it was Zachary who espe-

cially broke our hearts. He began audibly weeping as he moved
forward, but he didn't look back for us to save him.

I felt as if we were deserting him here in this foreign place. It
was all I could do not to scoop him up and take him back to
homeschool him and his brothers in our living room, where I
knew they would be safe and understood and loved.

Zachary is high-functioning, but he still has neurological issues.
Here he will be expected to perform as a regular first-grader without supports of any kind. As we drove home, Randy and I wondered whether we were putting him through too much, too soon.
I wanted to be optimistic, but I had strong doubts that this was
the appropriate educational placement for him.

I couldn't sleep all that night, and I wasn't the only one. For
the first time ever, Zachary cried himself to sleep. Why is he so
unhappy, so early? I wondered. He couldn't put it into words, and
I was left with worry as my companion throughout the long
night.

This educational confusion is in addition to a new medical
worry for Nicholas, who is due to have a biopsy in a few days
because of abnormal blood test results. The doctor told us that he
might have either polyps in his intestine or celiac disease, an in-
ability of the body to process wheat and other gluten foods. We
don't know which would be worse. If he has celiac disease, it's
likely that the other boys suffer from it, too, in which case we will
have to undertake a major reordering of all our diets. His biopsy
results could significantly change all of our lives depending on
what is found.

So here we are again, in the midst of new crises, in the thick of decisions that seem to never end. This is autism: always a work in progress, always full of adjustments and improvisation.

Like wrestlers, Randy and I have learned to roll with the punches. While we do not know what the future holds for our boys, we do know this: that we will be there with one arm urging them forward and the other ready to catch them if they fall.

APPENDICES

●   ●   ●

AUTISM RESOURCES

About.com: Autism
http://autism.about.com
A guide to diagnosing, treating, coping with, and thriving with autism.

AS Quarterly
http://www.asquarterly.com
Autism Spectrum Quarterly is a popular magazine published four times a year.

Autism Advocates
http://www.autismadvocates.com
An informative news and parent forum for families with autism.

Autism Collaboration

http://www.autism.org

A search engine that provides a path to treatment and recovery, and finds fact-based answers to your questions.

Autism Information Center

http://www.cdc.gov/ncbddd/autism

Information on autism provided by the U.S. Centers for Disease Control and Prevention.

Autism Link

http://www.autismlink.org

Website that gives information about current and upcoming events and conferences.

Autism One

http://www.autismone.org

A nonprofit organization started by a small group of parents of children with autism to address education, advocacy, and fund-raising.

Autism-PDD

http://www.autism-pdd.net

Informative website with various resources and parent forum on autism and pervasive developmental disorders.

Autism Podcast

http://www.autismpodcast.org

A weekly podcast website that interviews people from around the autism community with Mike and Lori Boll.

Autism Research Institute

http://www.autism.com

Since 1995, the Autsim Research Institute has convened meetings for researchers, physcians, and scientists committed to discovering effective treatment for autism, work that has become known as Defeat Autism Now!

Autism Resources

http://www.autism-resources.com

Information and links regarding the developmental disabilities autism and Asperger's syndrome.

Autism Society of America

http://www.autism-society.org

Dedicated to improving the lives of all those affected by autism.

Autism Source

http://autismsource.org

Online referral base of Autism Society of America—search engine designed to find local resources, providers, services, and support.

Autism Speaks

http://www.autismspeaks.org

Dedicated to funding research and increasing autism awareness, including diagnosis and treatment. Also provides connections to surveys and research.

AutismSpot

http://www.autismspot.com

Created by a father, this website emphasizes interactive features and provides video information and blogs "to offer support, hope, and encouragement through expert advice and community."

Autism United

http://www.autismunited.org

Autism United is a large group of families who are affected by autism.

Council of Parent Attorneys and Advocates (COPAA)

http://www.copaa.org

The Council of Parent Attorneys and Advocates provides information and seminars about special education for families with all types of disabilities.

Dan Marino Foundation

http://www.danmarinofoundation.org

Dan and Claire Marino established the Dan Marino Foundation to aid and assist families who have children with autism and special needs.

Dear Pharmacist

http://www.dearpharmacist.com

Pharmacist and syndicated columnist Suzy Cohen offers advice, with a particular focus on natural solutions and cutting-edge health treatments.

Doug Flutie Jr. Foundation for Autism
http://www.dougflutiejrfoundation.org

The Doug Flutie Jr. Foundation for Autism provides financial assistance for families who need it, and helps raise funds for research. Founded by Doug, a former NFL quarterback, and his wife, Laurie; their son Doug Jr. has autism.

Families with ASD
http://www.familieswithasd.org

Cincinnati-based autism group that holds an Autism Expo in Kentucky annually.

Generation Rescue
http://www.generationrescue.org

An international movement of scientists, physicians, and parent-volunteers helping more than fifteen thousand children begin biomedical treatment for autism.

HEAL! (Healing Every Autistic Life)
http://www.healautismnow.org

A community dedicated to medical research, treatment, and education of individuals, community awareness, and ultimately, prevention of autism spectrum disorders.

Healing Thresholds
http://autism.healingthresholds.com

Created to connect parents to autism therapy information as quickly and efficiently as possible, Healing Thresholds synthesizes a vast amount of complex information and links it with parental advice. Includes therapy fact sheets, research summaries, news summaries, and a community center.

IAN Research
http://www.ianresearch.org
IAN Research enables parents of children diagnosed with an Autism Spectrum Disorder (ASD) to participate in research over the Internet. Parents provide information about their child's diagnosis, behavior, family, environment, and services received.

Individuals with Disabilities Education Act (IDEA)
http://idea.ed.gov
IDEA ensures services to disabled children. IDEA also governs how states and public agencies provide early intervention, special education, and related services to more than 6.5 million eligible children.

National Autism Association (NAA)
http://www.nationalautismassociation.org
NAA is an organization that offers information and support to those affected by autism spectrum disorders

NICHCY
http://www.nichcy.org/Disabilities/Specific/Pages/Autism.aspx
National Dissemination Center for Children with Disabilities, one of four clearinghouses established by Congress to provide specialized information on disabilities.

NICHCY's Connections pages are designed to put you in quick contact with information that's readily available on the Internet.

Parents of Autistic Children (POAC)

http://www.poac.net

POAC, a group of families that help share information and resources.

Pathfinders for Autism

http://www.pathfindersforautism.org

Nonprofit run by baseball star B. J. Surhoff and his wife, Polly, for resources throughout Baltimore.

Project Lifesaver

http://www.projectlifesaver.org

Project Lifesaver provides a progressive approach to monitoring autistic children. In coordination with local law enforcement, Project Lifesaver can help track and recover children and adults who may be at risk of elopement.

Safe Minds

http://www.safeminds.org

The Coalition for Safe Minds (Sensible Action For Ending Mercury-Induced Neurological Disorders) is a private nonprofit organization founded to investigate and raise awareness of the risks to infants and children of exposure to mercury from medical products, including thimerosal in vaccines.

Schafer Autism Report (SAR)

http://www.sarnet.org

Monitors major news sources, websites, and the latest research for important and practical news and developments—sent out to your e-mail. (Available only by paid subscription.)

Dr. Stephen Shore—Asperger Autism

http://www.autismasperger.net

Dr. Shore's unique perspective on Asperger's syndrome. (Dr. Shore has Asperger's.)

Talk About Curing Autism (TACA)

http://www.talkaboutcuringautism.org

TACA provides information, resources, and support to families affected by autism. TACA aims to speed up the cycle time from the autism diagnosis to effective treatments.

Unlocking Autism

http://www.unlockingautism.org

This Christian awareness and education organization offers links to related sites, news, and articles. It was founded primarily for the purpose of increasing awareness about the disorder.

Wright's Law

http://www.wrightslaw.com

A website regarding parental advocacy and interpreting the IDEA.

AUTISM INTERVENTIONS

Autism Network for Dietary Intervention (ANDI)

http://www.autismndi.com
To help parents understand, implement, and maintain dietary intervention for their autistic children.

Autism Service Dogs of America (ASDA)

http://www.autismservicedogsofamerica.com
ASDA is a nonprofit that provides service dogs to families with autism.

Autism Treatment Center of America

http://www.autismtreatmentcenter.org
Home of the Son-Rise Treatment Program.

CARBONE CLINIC

http://www.carboneclinic.com

Website of Dr. Vincent Carbone, a leading board-certified behavioral analyst who also holds workshops worldwide.

DAN PRACTITIONERS

http://www.autism.com/dan/index.htm#practlist

For a list of clinicians who assist families with autistic children in pursuing the Defeat Autism Now! approach.

FLOORTIME FOUNDATION

http://www.floortime.org/

Features an online basic course on the Floortime Model (with Dr. Stanley Greenspan). The definitive resource for Floortime.

LOVAAS INSTITUTE

http://www.lovaas.com

Research-based psychology clinic specializing in developing and implementing behavior modification treatment programs for children with autism.

NORTH STAR DOGS

http://www.northstardogs.com

A nonprofit that breeds, trains, and places golden retrievers with families with adults and children with disabilities (including autism) and other physical challenges.

Picture Exchange Communication System (PECS)

http://www.pecs.com

The website features the PECS methods and the Pyramid Approach to Education as founded by Dr. Andy Bondy and Lori Frost.

Pyramid Educational Products

http://www.pyramidproducts.com

Consultants on PECS (Picture Exchange Communication System) and online store.

Relationship Development Intervention (RDI)

http://www.rdiconnect.com

Family-based therapy for people with autism, Asperger's syndrome, and PDD.

TEACCH

http://www.teacch.com/

Provides research, diagnostic evaluations, parent training, and support groups, as well as recreation groups and supported employment. A division of the Department of Psychiatry of the University of North Carolina at Chapel Hill.

RECOMMENDED READING

Attwood, Tony. *The Complete Guide to Asperger's Syndrome*. Philadelphia: Jessica Kingsley, 2008.

Drawing together case studies and personal stories, this book presents information on all aspects of Asperger's syndrome.

Barbera, Mary Lynch, and Tracy Rasmussen. *The Verbal Behavior Approach: How to Teach Children with Autism and Related Disorders*. Philadelphia: Jessica Kingsley, 2007.

A concise and intelligent tour of an effective intervention for autistic children through both speech and nonverbal communication.

Biel, Lindsey, and Nancy Peske. *Raising a Sensory Smart Child: The Definitive Handbook for Helping Your Child with Sensory Integration Issues*. New York: Penguin, 2005.

A guide to help parents, therapists, and teachers understand children who have sensory integration problems—that is, difficulty processing everyday sensations, and who exhibit unusual behaviors such as avoiding or seeking out touch, movement, sounds, and sights.

Bleach, Fiona. *Everybody Is Different: A Book for Young People Who Have Brothers or Sisters with Autism.* Shawnee Mission, KS: Autism Asperger, 2002.

Provides answers to the questions of brothers and sisters of young people on the autism spectrum, and advice on making family life more comfortable for everyone concerned.

Bondy, Andy, and Lori Frost. *A Picture's Worth: PECS and Other Visual Communication Strategies in Autism* (Topics in Autism). Bethesda, MD: Woodbine House, 2001.

Presents the Picture Exchange Communication System (PECS), a communication system that allows a child to use a picture (or series of pictures) to express his needs and desires without a prompt or cue from another person.

Brazelton, T. Berry, and Stanley I. Greenspan. *The Irreducible Needs of Children: What Every Child Must Have to Grow, Learn, and Flourish.* Cambridge, MA: Perseus, 2001.

Pediatrician Brazelton and child psychiatrist Greenspan unite to present a frank treatise on what children really need from their parents and from society.

Brazelton, T. Berry, and Joshua Sparrow. *Touchpoints, Three to Six: Your Child's Emotional and Behavioral Development.* Cambridge, MA: Perseus, 2002.

Pediatrician Brazelton and child psychologist Sparrow offer encouragement to guide parents through the developmental maze.

Edwards, Andreanna, and Tom Dineen. *Taking Autism to School.* Woodbury, NY: JayJo Books, 2002.

In this book, part of an illustrated series for children, autism is simplified and normalized.

Gerlach, Elizabeth. *Just This Side of Normal: Glimpses into Life with Autism.* Eugene, OR: Four Leaf Press, 1999.

One mother's personal account of helping her child with autism and the impact on her life.

Grandin, Temple. *Thinking in Pictures: And Other Reports from My Life with Autism.* New York: Vintage, 2006.

Animal scientist, Ph.D., and autistic person, Temple Grandin writes about how she managed to function and succeed in the outside world.

Grandin, Temple, and Margaret Scariano. *Emergence: Labeled Autistic.* New York: Warner Books, 1996.

About growing up with autism, written by a high-functioning author.

Gray, Carol. *The New Social Story Book: Illustrated Edition.* Arlington, TX: Future Horizons, 2000.

Contains Gray's innovative concepts to teach social and functional skills to children with autism.

Greenspan, Stanley, with Nancy Thorndike Greenspan. *First Feelings: Milestones in the Emotional Development of Your Baby and Child.* New York: Penguin, 1994.

Provides concrete options for understanding and dealing with perplexing behaviors of children.

Greenspan, Stanley, with Nancy Breslau Lewis. *Building Healthy Minds: The Six Experiences That Create Intelligence and Emotional Worth in Babies and Young Children.* Cambridge, MA: Da Capo Press, 2000.

Greenspan identifies six crucial developmental stages and the healthy interactions babies need to have with their caretakers.

Greenspan, Stanley, and Serena Wieder. *Engaging Autism: Using the Floortime Approach to Help Children Relate, Communicate, and Think.* Cambridge, MA: Da Capo Lifelong Books, 2006.

An essential guide to the Floortime approach for treating children with autism spectrum disorders. Includes guidance for parents navigating the controversies surrounding autism treatment.

Greenspan, Stanley, Serena Wieder, and Robin Simons. *The Child with Special Needs: Encouraging Intellectual and Emotional Growth.* Cambridge, MA: Perseus, 1998.

A resource for any parent, teacher, or therapist who interacts with children with disabilities.

Gutstein, Steven E., and Rachelle K. Sheely. *Relationship Development Intervention with Young Children: Social and Emotional Development Activities for Asperger Syndrome, Autism, PDD and NLD.* Philadelphia: Jessica Kingsley, 2002.

A comprehensive set of activities for children aged two through eight; emphasizes foundational skills such as social referencing, regulating behavior, conversational reciprocity and synchronized actions. A comprehensive website acts as companion to the book.

Jepson, Bryon, Katie Wright, and Jane Johnson. *Changing the Course of Autism: A Scientific Approach for Parents and Physicians.* Boulder, CO: Sentient, 2007.

A scholarly analysis of the controversy about vaccinations and autism, this book presents evidence to support the theory that the significant increase in the number of childhood vaccinations may be directly related to the dramatic increase in cases of autism in the United States and other developed countries.

Kaufman, Barry Neil, and Raun Kaufman. *Son-Rise: The Miracle Continues.* Tiburon, CA: H. J. Kramer, 1995

Continues the story of Raun, the autistic son of Barry Neil Kaufman, as he attends college and becomes part of the family's educational foundation.

Kephart, Beth. *A Slant of Sun: One Child's Courage.* New York: Quill, 1999.

A National Book Award finalist about a mother and her young autistic son.

Kirby, David. *Evidence of Harm: Mercury in Vaccines and the Autism Epidemic: A Medical Controversy.* New York: St. Martin's Griffin, 2006.

A *New York Times* reporter, Kirby provides a serious journalistic account of the controversial question of whether a mercury-containing preservative called thimerosal, commonly used in children's vaccines, caused a national epidemic of juvenile autism.

Kluth, Paula. *You're Going to Love This Kid! Teaching Students with Autism in the Inclusive Classroom.* Baltimore: Brookes, 2003.

A guide to understanding students with autism and including them fully in the classroom. Provides strategies and concepts to help educators create an inclusive environment for autistic students in both primary and secondary schools.

Koegel, Robert L., and Lynn Kern Koegel. *Pivotal Response Treatments for Autism: Communication, Social & Academic Development.* Baltimore: Brookes, 2006.

The Pivotal Response Treatment, which uses natural learning opportunities to target and modify key behaviors in children with autism, is clearly presented in this accessible book.

Leach, Penelope. *Your Baby and Child: From Birth to Age Five.* New York: Alfred A. Knopf, 1997

A book that highlights each developmental stage—newborn, settled baby, older baby, toddler, and young child—in terms of everyday care, including feeding, teething, growing, excreting, crying, sleeping, and playing.

Lears, Laurie. *Ian's Walk: A Story About Autism.* Morton Grove, IL: Albert Whitman, 1998.

A children's book that illustrates the challenges and joys of having a sibling with autism.

Leszl, Janet Lord. *A Pebble to Polish.* BookSurge, 2007.

A novel that chronicles a young single mother's heroic efforts to parent a child with autism.

Lewis, Lisa. *Special Diets for Special Kids.* Arlington, TX: Future Horizons, 1998.

A physician and mother of autistic children herself, Dr. Lewis offers examples of food allergies and intolerances that affect health and behavior in children with autism, and provides gluten/casein-free recipes.

Lovaas, Ivar O. *Teaching Individuals with Developmental Delays: Basic Intervention Techniques.* Austin, TX: Pro-Ed, 2002.

Lovaas, a professor of psychology at the University of California at Los Angeles (and director of the Lovaas Institute for Early Intervention) provides a theoretical overview of Lovaas-style treatment as well as a detailed description of its teaching techniques and goals.

Maurice, Catherine. *Let Me Hear Your Voice: A Family's Triumph over Autism.* New York: Ballantine, 1994.

The uplifting account of a mother of three who pulls two of her children out of autism and into a normal life through the use of applied behavior analysis.

McCandless, Jaquelyn. *Children with Starving Brains.* Putney, VT: Bramble Books, 2007.

This book, written by an experienced clinician, provides a treatment guide for parents and physicians based on the theory that autism is a complex biomedical illness resulting in brain malnutrition.

McCarthy, Jenny. *Louder Than Words.* New York: E. P. Dutton, 2007.

A famous TV personality deals with her son's autism diagnosis and treatment, focusing on healing and hope.

McElwain, Jason J-Mac. *The Game of My Life: A True Story of Challenge, Triumph, and Growing Up Autistic.* New York: NAL Hardcover, 2008.

The inspiring true story of a high-school basketball player's triumph over the challenges of autism—and his opponents on the basketball court.

Miller, Lucy Jane, and Doris A. Fuller. *Sensational Kids: Hope and Help for Children with Sensory Processing Disorder.* New York: Perigee, 2007.

Presents symptoms of SPD and its four major subtypes, ways the disorder is diagnosed and treated, and sensory strategies for living with the condition.

Naseef, Robert. *Special Children, Challenged Parents: The Struggles and Rewards of Raising a Child with a Disability.* Baltimore, MD: Brookes, 2001.

A candid portrayal of the challenges of raising a disabled or seriously ill child.

Notbohm, Ellen. *Ten Things Every Child with Autism Wishes You Knew.* Arlington, TX: Future Horizons, 2005.

For social workers, teachers, and relatives of children with autism, this book uses the unique perspective of a child's voice to help us understand the thinking patterns of autistic children so that we can communicate with them in meaningful ways.

Notbohm, Ellen, and Veronica Zysk. *Ten Things Your Student with Autism Wishes You Knew.* Arlington, TX: Future Horizons, 2006.

Again using the unique perspective of an autistic child's voice, this book is geared toward teachers.

Parish, Robert, ed. *Embracing Autism: Connecting and Communicating with Children in the Autism Spectrum.* Hoboken, NJ: Jossey-Bass, 2008.

Designed to help those working with autistic children better understand their world, provide insights into what makes them tick, and offer useful information on how they communicate, learn, and succeed.

Robison, John Elder. *Look Me in the Eye: My Life with Asperger's.* New York: Three Rivers Press, 2008.

This memoir compellingly explains the challenges in growing up with Asperger's in the days before the syndrome even had a name.

Senator, Susan. *Making Peace with Autism: One Family's Story of Struggle, Discovery, and Unexpected Gifts.* Trumpeter, 2006.

This mother's narrative offers strategies and wisdom for handling the daily challenges of raising a child with autism.

Seroussi, Karyn, and Bernard Rimland. *Unraveling the Mystery of Autism and Pervasive Developmental Disorder: A Mother's Story of Research and Recovery.* New York: Broadway Books, 2002.

The author became a crusader for dietary intervention after diet change made a remarkable difference in the condition of her own autistic son. Seroussi is cofounder of ANDI (the Autism Network for Dietary Intervention) and coeditor of the *ANDI News.*

Shaw, William. *Biological Treatments for Autism and PDD.* Toronto: Sunflower, 2001.

An accessible guide to a wide range of therapies that have proved useful in autism treatment, including antifungal and antibacterial therapies, gluten and casein restriction, homeopathy, vitamin therapy, gamma globulin treatment, transfer factor therapies, and treatment of food allergies.

Shore, Stephen, and Linda Rastelli. *Understanding Autism for Dummies.* Hoboken, NJ: For Dummies, 2006.

This book explains the differences between various types of autism and delivers crucial information on behavioral, educational, medical, and other interventions.

Siegel, Bryna. *Helping Children with Autism Learn: Treatment Approaches for Parents and Professionals.* New York: Oxford University Press, 2007.

Accessible to both parents and teachers, this book provides concise and easy-to-understand information on educating an autistic child.

Siegel, Lawrence M. *The Complete IEP Guide: How to Advocate for your Special Ed Child.* Berkeley: NOLO, 2004.

Spells out the IEP process in easy-to-follow steps.

Twachtman-Cullen, Diane, Jennifer Twachtman-Reilly, and David L. Holmes. *How Well Does Your IEP Measure Up? Quality Indicators for Effective Service Delivery.* Higganum, CT: Starfish Specialty Press, 2002.

A practical guide to developing an IEP that optimizes service delivery to an autistic child. Key legal issues are also discussed.

Waltz, Mitzi. *Autistic Spectrum Disorders: Understanding the Diagnosis and Getting Help.* Sebastopol, CA: Patient Center Guides, 2002.

A patient advocate incorporates current medical findings on treatment and possible causes for ASDs.

Weber, Jayne Dixon. *Children with Fragile X Syndrome: A Parent's Guide.* Bethesda, MD: Woodbine House, 2000.

An introduction to Fragile X syndrome written for parents and families.

White, Burton L. *The First Three Years of Life*, 20th rev. ed. New York: Fireside, 1995.

A child development classic, covering the first three years of life.

Wilens, Timothy E. *Straight Talk About Psychiatric Medications for Kids.* New York: Guilford Press, 2004.

A practical guide that arms parents with the knowledge to understand risks, benefits, and role of psychiatric medications for children.

Wiseman, Nancy. *Could It Be Autism? A Parent's Guide to the First Signs and Next Steps.* New York: Broadway Books, 2006.

Contains an easy-to-use checklist, as well as detection and intervention strategies for developmental delays.

Wright, Peter. *Wrightslaw: From Emotions to Advocacy: The Special Education Survival Guide.* Hartfield, VA: Harbor House Law Press, 2006.

This comprehensive book instructs parents how to plan, prepare, and obtain quality special-education services.

ACKNOWLEDGMENTS

To Lynn's mom, Jean, and youngest sister, Lori, thank you both for showing the boys unconditional love and always being there to lend a loving hand.

Our sincerest gratitude to our literary agent, Janis Vallely, who helped bring our story to life and helped us navigate the publishing world. To Lynn Lauber, whose writing skills and editorial expertise made it possible for us to write this book, we could not have done it without you. To our editor, Lucia Watson, thanks for believing in our book enthusiastically and making it a reality. To Lisa Johnson and Anne Kosmoski, thanks for helping to get the word out and for raising awareness about the book. Thanks to Mirian Rich for your hard work and enthusiasm, and to Megan Newman for the opportunity of a lifetime.

Thanks to Dr. Mark A. Young for friendship and assistance, to Lisa Miles for believing in Autism Expo, and to Shannon Roberts for being the teacher every child with autism deserves.

A special thank-you to the following therapists, teachers, and aides: Shannon Barrett, Michael Bell, Nicole Brown, Linda Carter-Ferrier, Jennifer Cleckner, Nancy Davis, Julia DeMino, Mary Dokos, Heather Dvoskin, Candace Felske, Jennifer Harwood, Steven Josephson, Carmella Loomis, Annette Myers, Laurie O'Connell, Alfreda Pryor, Annette Read, Renee Suss, Pam Vogel, Marian Wheltle, and Diane Zoeller.

Our gratitude to the following friends and coworkers: Kathy Bennett, Stephen Bounds, Michele Brickley, Gordon Clifford, Roy Conley, Steve and Mary James, Greg Kilduff, Lily and Liz Kilduff, Lois Kishel, Debby Lomax, John Magoon, John O'Donoghue, Tracy Oldaker, Lisa Spencer, and John Woolums.

Thanks to the people who donated their free time and helped make Autism Expo 2007 a success: Dr. Regina Carney, Dr. Pamela Compart, Dr. Janelle Love, Dr. Kathy Niager, Dr. Stephen Shore, and Dr. Susan Swedo; and Jennifer Bobbitt, Rae Anne Brodie-Kaylie, Scott Campbell, Brandy Colby, Nikia Dower, Heather Franks, Susan Hayward, Michelle Hurst, Melissa Lebowitz, Gretchen Levine, Mark B. Martin, Esq., Sherry Moyer, Cynthia Onder, Julia and Greg Smith, and Tara Wagner.

Thanks to the attendees, vendors, and volunteers who supported the Autism Expo (too many to name here personally).

To all the doctors, teachers, therapists, and aides whom we have met throughout the years who are not named, we send our gratitude.

INDEX